Young,
Sober
& Free

About the Book

Young, Sober & Free sets forth practically and cogently in disarming, perhaps even irreverent fashion at times, the harsh truth about mind-affecting chemicals and young people. Shelly Marshall and her young collaborators relate the personal experiences of those who have lived through addiction. By sharing experiences, strengths, and hopes, those youths who will suffer from the addiction to alcohol and related drugs may begin to find a way to sobriety and freedom.

The work also furnishes a clear picture of the primary tools of recovery—the Twelve Steps of Alcoholics Anonymous. The Twelve Steps are a group of principles, spiritual in their nature, which, if practiced as a way of life, can expel the obsession to drink and enable the sufferer to become happily and usefully whole.

All authorities involved in the treatment of alcoholism recognize that regardless of whatever therapeutic approaches may be necessary in individual cases, unless they serve as a bridge to A.A., they are unlikely to be effective over a long period of time. Regardless of what anyone may think of the spiritual program of recovery of A.A., over one million recovering alcoholics can testify to a very practical truth: it works. No other method, technique or program comes close to its success.

Young,
Sober
& Free

Written and compiled by
Shelly Marshall

 HAZELDEN®

The life stories in this book were written by the young men and women whose first names they bear. The remainder of the material in the book was written by Shelly Marshall.

The Twelve Steps of Alcoholics Anonymous, © *1976 Alcoholics Anonymous World Services, Inc. Reprinted with permission.*

The Twelve Steps of Narcotics Anonymous, © *1976 Narcotics Anonymous World Service Organization, Inc. Reprinted with permission.*

The Twelve Steps of the Palmer Drug Abuse Program, © *1972 The Palmer Drug Abuse Program, Inc. Reprinted with permission.*

First published, September, 1978

ISBN: 0-89486-055-0
Library of Congress Catalog Card Number: 78:060061

Printed in the United States of America

CONTENTS

About the Author

Shelly Marshall has worked with alcoholic and drug addicted youth for six years as a counselor and, more importantly, as a friend. Most recently, she worked at St. Luke's Hospital in Denver, Colorado, in the Alcohol Rehabilitation Unit.

At present, she is living soberly and freely in Priest River, Idaho, where she continues to write for and about her young chemically dependent friends as she works on building her own home in the mountains.

Foreword

Over a million men and women, once stricken with the critical disease of alcoholism and/or addiction, now glowingly speak in almost every tongue of their personal miracle of recovery through the fellowships of Alcoholics Anonymous and Narcotics Anonymous.

Of the millions still suffering, there is a tragic, dying group of people formerly overlooked or actually denied help. They comprise the thousands of chemically-dependent teenagers who need these programs for their survival. We have heard their voices; we have heard their cries . . . not once, but a thousand times. As the diseases of alcoholism and other addictions are no respecters of race, religion, or social status, they are also no respecters of age. We have written this book to reach out to our young fellow sufferers in the hope that they may accept help, thereby avoiding years of suffering, heartache, and premature death.

In the words we have set down in this book, "We only repeat what has been given us by the Fellowships of A.A. and N.A." It is *not* our intention to write a new program or begin a new fellowship. Our message is a supplement to the existing books and literature of both Fellowships tailored specifically to young people. We remember always that we are members of A.A., N.A., and the Palmer Drug Abuse Program, and that any controversies are to be settled within our home groups through group conscience.

We have found a way and wish to share—not to make rules, not to start a cult—but if you find you can use our model of sobriety, we welcome you and hope you experience our joy in being *Young, Sober and Free.*

Acknowledgment

We would like to acknowledge the many young
people, professionals, parents, and members of
A.A. and N.A. who so generously wrote for this
book. We couldn't list all those who
contributed either directly or indirectly to
these pages, but we would like to
acknowledge one person officially:

Judge Jim Hale
whose personal motto impresses us,

"I ain't preaching . . . ."

Introduction

*"We never want to be trapped in the prison
of closed-mindedness or rigidity—
it reminds us too much of our disease."*
Shelly Marshall

A few months ago, I went to Saint Luke's Hospital on a Sunday morning to make rounds on the Alcoholism Recovery Unit. At that particular time, we had a rather large percentage of young alcoholics and drug abusers—middle and late teens and early twenties. A rather typical young couple—he had nice shoulder-length blonde hair while she had closely cropped darker hair, both wearing cut-off blue jeans and barefeet—came strolling by, hand-in-hand. In response to my greeting and question they said they were going down to the main lobby for a newspaper. Almost instinctively I thought: "Not in my nice clean hospital, you're not!"

For reasons not known to me at that time, I repressed my impulse and let them go on. Later, in evaluating my feelings, it occurred to me that much of my life as a doctor, father, and teacher had been spent in passing on messages from the critical parent ego state which had been incorporated into my own value judgments with little regard for the true values involved. Who was I to decide if the precepts of middle-aged dress codes should be forced on the youth of today? Aside from a certain amount of protection and warmth, what other universal values do shoes have? I felt elated that such a simple discovery could free me from the need to defend ideas which were not truly principles.

A few weeks later my new found freedom was reinforced when one of our hospital administrators came to me with a complaint that some of our patients were walking through an adjoining section of the hospital in their barefeet. Without blinking an eye and the barest trace of a smile, I was able to tell him that we had done a scientific study comparing the scrapings of the soles of the shoes of thirty-nine consecutive white, middle-class, middle-aged, American Protestants with the scrapings from the bare soles of our young people and could find no difference. There have been no further complaints.

I use this personal experience in introducing this new book, *Young, Sober and Free,* because it relates to the style Ms. Marshall has used in intertwining recognition of disease processes with specific recommendations for recovery and wrapping up the whole nicely with the strongest of all binders, the personal experiences of those who have lived through it, the sharing of experiences, strengths, and hopes so that those youths who still suffer from the addictions to alcohol and related drugs may begin to find a way to sobriety and freedom.

While the message in this book is directed mainly to the young sufferer, there is material for all who are concerned with the problem. Certainly, any physician involved with care of the youth of today, be he family practitioner, pediatrician, school health officer, or psychiatrist, will benefit from the knowledge it imparts, if for no other reason than to prepare himself for the questions it will raise in the minds of his patients and their families. It will be a helpful book for educators, psychologists, counselors, social workers, and law enforcement personnel, each of whom must deal with the problem of addiction on a daily and interpersonal basis. Perhaps most importantly, it will be of great value to the parents and families of the youth of our country who puzzle, pray, and ponder over the dual dilemma: "Is my loved one an alcoholic or an addict?" And if so, "What do I do about it?"

In their attempt to answer these questions, Ms. Marshall and her young collaborators have combined two of the most effective tools available— experience and the Twelve Steps of recovery of Alcoholics Anonymous. They tell us this truth: "If mind-affecting chemicals create problems in your life and you keep using them for any reason, then you have a problem with mind-affecting chemicals." Truth is truth, and by whatever process it is arrived at, it is what it is, or it is not truth. The truth presented in this book is practical and hard-hitting; it is presented in a disarming and attention-holding, albeit somewhat irreverent manner.

"I had one of those normal childhoods. You know the kind—full of loneliness, insecurity, remorse, fear, low self-esteem, and dishonesty." Perhaps no place in the book draws attention to the practical truth so compellingly as: "We can analyze, rationalize, and intellectualize our way into or out of just about anything. So we ask you to stop the intellectual crap and just work the steps. Judge the results later; don't try to know the results first. You can't, you really can't. If we've learned nothing else we have learned this about life: You can analyze it to death.''

The "Steps" referred to in the above passage are the Twelve Steps of recovery which are presented in the book *Alcoholics Anonymous* written by the fellowship of the same name. A.A., as exemplified in its Twelve Steps, is recognized as the single most-effective force in the treatment of the disease of alcoholism. Most authorities involved in the treatment of alcoholism recognize that regardless of what therapeutic approaches may be necessary in individual cases, unless they serve as a bridge to A.A., they are unlikely to be effective over a long period of time. Regardless of what anyone may think of the spiritual program of recovery of A.A., over one million recovered alcoholics can testify to a very practical truth: "It works." No other method, technique, or program comes close to its success.

Some purists, both in the field of alcoholism and medicine, may object to these young people combining the diseases of alcoholism and drug addictions into the same syndrome.

But no less an authority than Stanley Gitlow, M.D., an authority on alcoholism and the pharmacology and physiology of related problems, has suggested the term "sedativism" to cover the effects of many of the drugs which have cross-addiction and cross-tolerance with alcohol. We do recognize that for alcoholics the use of any of these drugs is a guarantee of failure as far as sobriety is concerned. Gitlow has stated that "trying to reinforce the urge the alcoholic has to cure all of his problems by taking something by mouth is doomed to failure." Although modified somewhat by acceptance of deterrents such as disulfiram (antabuse), this dictum is accepted as valid by nearly all authorities and most extend it also to drugs administered by parenteral injection or inhalation. Of course, it must be recognized that we are speaking here only of mind-affecting chemicals and not potentially life-saving medications such as insulin, antibiotics, and cardiac medications.

In poking their pins into the prideful balloons of some self-appointed experts from the various learned disciplines, Ms. Marshall et al have not spared their peers. "Just because you're a space-case doesn't automatically place others in the stoneage. In reality, our closed-mindedness has just trapped inside of us what little we know, mainly because we so egotistically think we know it all. One cannot be taught anything new if he already knows it all." Those of us who are recognized as card-carrying members-in-good-standing of the Establishment would point out that fact and be met by an attitude such as, "My parents graciously shared their objections with me.

That's when I built the brick walls, building them higher and higher, so as not to hear their too-loud voices and over-dramatic lectures. Stone-faced, I hid behind those walls, denying and lying to their questions and accusations." Regardless of the reason for building the walls, whether to keep something in or to keep something out, the builder must spend all of his time defending the wall. What better way of breaching the wall than to have a peer trumpet: "Coming off as a goody two-shoes? What's so great about coming off as a bad-ass?" And parents are treated kindly: "Keep in mind, our parents weren't always wrong, though it was easier for us to think that than to look at ourselves."

Throughout this book runs a strain of spirituality that will disturb some, but remains true spirituality nonetheless. Despite the stories of sex (both straight and gay), prostitution, rape, incest, violence, and theft, these young people have tried to present a common thread of hope based on spiritual growth. "It is apparent that our common bond is not in the disease, but in the solution. We have found the same way out." The "way out" is that referred to in the book *Alcoholics Anonymous:* God is doing for us what we could not do for ourselves." For those who may find some of the language offensive, I urge you not to let this interfere with your reception of the underlying message. Marty Mann, founder of the National Council on Alcoholism, says: "The Alcoholic does not hear what you say. He feels what you feel." Try to feel what these young people are saying. "For this change in my life I'm gratefull to A.A., but I thank God, for only He could have done what no others were able to do." We recognize our own need to place our dependence on God in the treatment of alcoholism and related dependency diseases, and this presents some interesting experiences.

Some time ago, a psychiatrist from our hospital—a detractor of our work —asked me: "Larry, how come you have success with these people and I don't?" I said: "It's very simple. I believe in God." He said: "Don't give me any of that!" I said: "I don't have anything else to give you."

"We have attempted in this book to share our own model of sobriety with you in the hope that you will face the light, thus allowing the shadows to fall behind."

—Shelly Marshall

Larry Gibson, M.D.
Director, Alcoholism Recovery Unit
St. Luke's Hospital, Denver, Colorado

Never Too Young

"It's a good thing I'm not too young to be an alcoholic," I probably wouldn't live long enough to become old enough."
Teddy

At the present time, knowledge about the disease of alcoholism and other addictions remains sketchy. We know that the disease is fatal if it is not interrupted. We know that a person may drink or use for many years and all of a sudden fall apart physically or psychologically. We know that there are people who are heavy drinkers, but who are not alcoholics. We know that how much a person drinks or how often a person drinks isn't what makes a person alcoholic.

But there are a lot of things that we don't know for sure. We don't know exactly how a person becomes an alcoholic. We don't know exactly how to predict which persons will become alcoholic and which ones won't. And we don't know how to cure an alcoholic; we don't even know for sure if an alcoholic can be cured.

Not too many years ago, a lot of people thought that alcoholics were men (no one wanted to believe that women could be drunks) who had lost their jobs, their families, and even a decent place to live. An alcoholic lived on skid row. People certainly didn't believe that someone as young as fifteen or sixteen could be an alcoholic. Today we know better.

The fact that the disease exists among those under twenty-five is not in question by those of us young people who have it; only by those, both young and old, who would charge us with "moral weakness," "lack of will power," or just general "bad characters." These ill-informed, sometimes well-meaning, individuals speak of us as being too nice, too smart, or too young to be an alcoholic. We know better and will attempt to explain what we have learned about our disease for the benefit of you who are asking, "Am I or am I not an alcoholic or an addict?" and "What do I do about it?"

Our attitudes and chances toward recovery depend greatly on how we define and understand the disease we are recovering from. If you believe:

- Even if I have to stop drinking, I can still smoke grass because it's non-addictive;
- I can stop using for a few years, get my head together, and then be able to have a couple drinks now and again;
- Alcoholism and drug addiction are two different things;
- I'm too young; after all, my parents have been drinking for years;

then you don't yet understand the complex nature of our illness. But you are not alone. Many people do not yet understand addiction, and it was only through hard falls, study, time, and a lot of effort that we reached a basic understanding of the magnitude and difficulty of what we are dealing with. Many will not agree with us. And that is all right, they are entitled to their opinion. However, it is our lives and freedom that are endangered, not others'. It is not without careful consideration and much prayer that we explore this disease with you.

Today, it seems, everyone is an expert when it comes to talking about drinking and drugs. And a lot of people use words that mean one thing to them, but quite another to someone else. For purposes of simplicity, when speaking of our disease, the words *alcoholic, addict, chemically dependent, pill head, pot head,* etc. will be used interchangeably. We refer to the same thing: what we have labelled the addictions syndrome (affectionately known. in our group as the "ass disease").

The word that probably needs a comment is the word *syndrome. Syndrome* just means a group of concurrent things that form a usually identifiable pattern. The things that occur together are some physical things, some mental things, and some spiritual things. What we see in young people who are hooked on a chemical is a physical compulsion, a mental obsession, and a lack of spirituality—call it self-centeredness. The disease is marked by a compulsive use of substances, powerlessness over what they do, an impairment of the normal state of health that interferes with our thrust for life and joy in living—all disguised as "better living through chemistry."

The first part of the addictions syndrome is the physical compulsion. This compulsion can perhaps best be described as the body craving drugs, possibly even to its own destruction. When you have that craving, your brain may or may not give its o.k. You know you shouldn't have another fix, pill, or drink,and maybe you really don't want to have another. But the craving is there—probably along with some fear and some physical pain or jumpiness. You may have things you would rather be doing. But you take that first drink or pill—and it isn't enough. You want another, then another. And the compulsion is off and running one more time. Thus, we know it's the *first* fix, pill, or drink that gets us stoned, not the fourth, tenth, or sixteenth. One of our group remarked, "A compulsion is being trapped in a known destructive reality. It's a dead-end space. And we walk right into it." We agree.

There are four major categories for the mind-affecting chemicals:

Sedatives (e.g., librium, barbiturates, quaalude, alcohol)

Narcotics (e.g., morphine, heroin, methadone)

Stimulants (e.g., diet pills, speed, amphetamines)

Hallucinogenics (e.g., LSD, peyote, marijuana)

Experts agree that sedatives, narcotics, and stimulants are highly addictive. We will not enter into the scientific controversy over the addictive or non-addictive properties of hallucinogenics. However, we are reminded of the guy who, when asked if grass was addicting, replied, "It *can't* be, I've smoked it every day for five years!"

It is known that once a person is addicted to any one of the drugs in a particular category, he has a built-up tolerance for *any* drug in that same category, and a built-up tolerance is the first stage of ADDICTION. Tolerance means that it takes more and more of a drug to do the same thing it used to. If you began doing a little heroin and got high, as time went on you had to do a little more and a little more to get high. Your body became tolerant to narcotics. This means that if you go to the hospital in severe pain, it is going to take more morphine to relieve the pain than it would for the average person who has not built up a tolerance. The same with sedatives. If you are dependent on tranquilizers and have developed a tolerance for them, you'll also need more alcohol to get high, whether you drink often or not. Theoretically, a person can be an alcoholic without *ever* having had a drink of alcohol.

Many physicians, medical researchers, and others believe that people can be born with tolerances. Dr. Larry Gibson, the writer of the preface of this book and Director of the alcohol and drug unit at St. Luke's Hospital in Denver, says that most teenage alcoholics seem to be born with the physical tolerance part of alcoholism because they simply haven't had the time to break down their systems. We know personally of four nine-year olds throughout the country who have been treated for chronic alcoholism.

Whatever the bio-chemical or genetic roots are, we do know that once you have it, you have it for life, and it is chronic, progressive, and fatal.

"Well, o.k.," a person says, "I agree that I'm addicted to alcohol, and I believe that sedatives will trigger my compulsion, but there's no reason why I can't smoke pot or snort a little coke." Ah, yes. This is a thought many of us have entertained, sometimes till we had no thoughts left at all. Remember, we are dealing with a disease larger than just the physical component. We also have the mental obsession.

Mentally, we are high chasers. Most of us would rather feel happy than sad; we like to feel that our body and mind are working together perfectly. We like to feel smooth and easy. For many of us—probably all of us—there was a lot of pain and boredom in our lives. We wanted something better, but we didn't always know how to get what we wanted. We just wanted to feel better. Right in the front of our brains was the obsession with the idea of getting high, escaping reality, or being somewhere other than where we really were. So what is bad about that?

Nothing. Wanting that dizzy-light-somewhere-else feeling is not bad. So many people have that desire that it's safe to call it completely natural. Even kids have it. Observe children at a playground; the thrill of a merry-go-round is actually that dizzy-light-somewhere-else feeling. How about kids holding their breath trying to faint, or spinning in circles till they lose their balance? What about the most popular rides at an amusement park? Young people can have as much pain and boredom in their lives as somebody who lives to be a hundred, and just as much, they can want to be rid of it.

So we don't think that the feelings we search for are sick or unnatural. However, our wires got tangled up somewhere along the neural pathway, because in our use of alcohol and other drugs, we keep seeking even when the good feelings these chemicals give have disappeared; we keep seeking even when our use is obviously self-destructive; when we can't remember the trip, when drinking or using gets us into serious trouble, when people don't like us anymore. We keep seeking even when we knew that we had lost control. We *try* and *try* and *try*, conning ourselves with, "This time it'll be different; I got into trouble because of my stupid friends (parents, police, circumstances, the dog — whatever). I'll smoke grass instead of drink; I'll pop pills instead of using a needle, or snort coke instead of anything." This is the point at which we should recognize our compulsion, but we seldom do.

The mental obsession we have about our drinking or using may not seem crazy at the time, but when we look back at it, it doesn't seem to be very sane.

We know from past experience that when we drink or take drugs, bad things happen to us. Yet here we are, one more time, reaching for that first fix, pill, or drink, ready to drop into the old compulsion again. Against all odds, we feel that somewhere, somehow, something has got to work and we will find the magic drug or working combination of drugs and alcohol if we just try hard enough and experiment long enough. What we won't admit to anybody or ourselves—perhaps because we just don't quite know it at the time—is that consciousness expanders, relaxers, uppers, downers, all of them are brain scramblers for us. But we keep trying, and we keep getting knocked around by the very things we are using to try to make our lives a little better. We are preoccupied with getting high because we feel that it is the solution to all our problems.

In its own way, our crazy searching after the high through the use of alcohol and other drugs makes a certain kind of sense. To a person, every addict and alcoholic is a very self-centered individual. We are conscious of our needs, our desires, our problems, our abilities—and our shortcomings. In short, we are self-centered people. Any working connection with a loving creative Power or the forces of the universe is practically non-existent in our lives. We are definitely not spiritual people. Our reliance is in chemicals, not in God. How we got this way is not always clear, and in a way, it is not very important for us to figure out why we are so self-centered.

But most of us have enough honesty to figure out that if we rely solely on our own powers, if we rely solely on ourselves, we won't have a very happy or fulfilling life. Maybe we feel that we aren't worth attention from God or from other people. Maybe we feel that we are, but that we just don't get it. Then, because we lack a good, solid connection with a Greater Power, we turn to chemicals to give us what we know we need; we feel compelled to use drugs. And the result is that we just become more turned in on ourselves. Our self-centeredness grows.

Sooner or later the addict and the alcoholic find themselves in a sad state. They have a compulsion to drink and use, even when they don't want to; things they want to do and people they want to be with come second—a distant second—to drinking or using the drugs; they have only themselves to rely on. They have become loners through their self-centeredness. So what comes next?

Here are the steps that worked for us. Knowing what we now know about our disease, we begin Step One:

**Step 1:   We admitted that we were powerless over our addiction, that
our lives had become unmanageable.**

"But I'm not powerless," is the cry of most beginners. One of our people
described it this way:

"I had a hard time accepting the idea that I was an alcoholic because
when I would drink, I might not lose control that particular time. But it
would start a process in me that I couldn't stop. To be an alcoholic, I
thought, I had to drink a beer, and five days later find myself with no
money in a cheap hotel in another state. I saw that as powerlessness.
Then I realized that I had absolutely no power in stopping my downward
slide into trouble; my gradual intake of alcohol became greater, and my
ill feelings towards myself and others grew. I didn't feel this way
because I wanted to. I tried not to, but I simply couldn't control it and
that showed me powerlessness, but only after I was sober awhile."

The terms "alcoholic" and "addict" have differing connotations for many
people, so it is important to accept the general concept of powerlessness
before pinning a label on yourself that you may not fully believe or
understand. On the whole, we don't fret about labels like *pot head, pill head,
alcoholic,* or *junkie.* The kind of drug we were hooked on is not very important.
We just admit our powerlessness over intoxicants. Either we are or we aren't;
there is no middle ground. Either our way with chemicals worked or it didn't,
and if it didn't, we found our lives unmanageable. But we didn't accept
"unmanageability" without some problems. At this point, a lot of people fall
into the trap of comparison and become what we've coined the "not yets."
Another of our group explains the trap like this:

"I had a certain definition in my mind of an addict. First, it was a person
who acted like a different person while stoned—that hadn't happened
to me yet. When it did, an addict became someone who was getting into
car wrecks.That hadn't happened to me yet, then it did. It went on. An
addict was someone who was late and delinquent in school, then a drop
out, then someone who couldn't remember the night before, etc. As I
hit each level, my definition of an addict kept going to the next level
down."

Anytime we compare ourselves to others in deciding whether or not we
have a problem, we will always find those worse off than we are. We can
always use the comparison to our advantage so that we look good, so that we
are cool or hip. The only valid comparison is that of ourselves to ourselves

over a period of time. Am I better today than I was yesterday? Am I better this month as compared to last month or last year?

There are other questions we can ask ourselves in determining our own addiction: Do mind-affecting chemicals affect the way I feel about myself, my friends, the people around me? Do I seem to be in a downward trap? The point is *not*, "Am I an alcoholic?" but, "Can I drink and take dope and be peaceful with my life as a whole?" The addictions syndrome is a progressive disease. It gets worse, never better, and the "not yets" are people for whom the only question is one of time.

The members of the group have decided that since we have identified the problem today, we will work on the solution today. Why wait for years on down the road *after* we're permanently institutionalized, or have gone through two or three families, or wreaked havoc in the lives of many? We have heard and can learn from the experience of those in A.A. and N.A. Contrary to what you might think, waiting does not add years to the fun of partying and getting high. It adds years to the disaster and heartache. If you live through those years. Many of our peers *died* in that car wreck that we survived just by luck. They *died* from an accidental overdose, some do have a brain like a vegetable from the once-too-often, or suffocated from their last glue trip. Yes, it really does happen, and yes, it can happen to you.

We might remind you that no one goes to jail, drops out of school, or gets pregnant from eating peanut butter. If mind-affecting chemicals create problems in your life and you keep using them for *whatever* reasons, then you have a problem with mind-affecting chemicals. Since you are reading this book, we will also point out that people who do not have a problem with alcohol or other drugs seldom question or worry about whether they do.

CINDY

She's seventeen and has three years sobriety.

At fourteen I was lucky, I found help. I always pictured an alcoholic as a male, approximately seventy years old, who slept in gutters and on park benches, and carried a cheap bottle of whiskey around in a brown paper sack. Today, when I think of someone who fits that description, I have to laugh. Boy, was I wrong!

I started drinking when I was about three years old. Oh, not real drinking, but that is when I got my start. My dad used to let me have sips of his beer. I would lift the bottle up, put it to my lips, open my throat, and let it pour. I was chug-a-lugging at three! I would then hand the half-empty bottle back to my dad, walk through the door, and promptly fall flat on my face. I was a real adult.

In these early moments of drinking, I discovered something that urged me on in my drinking career. When I drank I felt that I fit right in with the adults and I was comfortable. I also found that everyone liked me and that I received a lot of attention.

By the time I was five, I was allowed to drink a whole bottle or two, if I could hold that much beer, and I began to learn to plan, eventually planning how I would manage to sneak an extra bottle or how to smuggle some beer into my lunch thermos to take to school.

From then on much of my life is a blank. I remember I had a mean first grade teacher, a nice second grade teacher, and I was bombed in third grade. By fifth grade I would get the shakes when I couldn't find booze. I lived in a fantasy world with make-believe parents in a make-believe place. In sixth grade I finally found friends (and enemies). I found a few people who drank and we quickly became buddies. I also recall getting in fights with kids and teachers because I was loud, rude, and obnoxious. At those times, I always got sent out to sit on the steps, and I loved it, because all of the "cool" people would be on the steps and I wanted to be one of the cool ones.

In the next two years, my drinking changed, and so did my life. I discovered a new, large group of friends and a new, large world of drugs. Many things happened during this time. My parents were separated, I was suspended from school, busted for shop-lifting; I delved heavily into drugs, started pushing drugs, and totally withdrew. In school I didn't have a book locker, I had a liquor cabinet. I joined a gang of kids who practically ran the school, and there were some pretty large guys who would protect me from harm. All of this was really cool. In this situation, I tried many different drugs and became addicted to many. Reality began to fade in and out for me.

My mother would come to me with all her sorrows over my dad and many times I wished I could tell her to bug off. Some days the divorce was on, then it was off, and then on again. This went on for what seemed like years, yet in a way it was unreal. I lived in my own dimension and *nothing* seemed concrete. I fantasized about everything. My world appeared to be different from the outside world and, in looking back, there was not even a glint of reality in the world of my creation.

I seemed to form two separate personalities. At times I would wish someone would put me away. I thought I was crazy and many times I dreamed of death. Depression became so heavy that I wanted to take my life, but I became too apathetic to take any action on it. I couldn't sleep without help, and help came in taking pills in outrageous amounts to put me on my way.

One day, just to get through the school day, I accidentally took an overdose of pills. I never knew what those pills were, but I took too many. Along came strange visions, and in panic, I began pulling out my hair. By the end of the day I had bald spots on my head and I was so weak that I had to be carried home. By this time I had had quite a few experiences with blackouts. People were always telling me what a good time I had at a party that I didn't even know I had been at. It frightened me when I came to in places I had never been before. That something might be wrong with me, I began to suspect, but I was still far from admitting it.

At last, a friend conned me into going to the Palmer Drug Abuse Program. When I first went, I found the people had something I wanted, so I hung around and really thought I could get their happiness through osmosis. I tried to stay straight and it worked, for awhile.

Then, suddenly, it all changed. One day my parents told my brother and me that we were moving to Denver. It seemed like not even a week went by before we were packed and on the road. I hated Denver and I hated the people there, but in an effort to show my friends back home in Houston how well I was doing, I tried to stay straight. It seemed to me that I could turn over a new leaf and finally be the person I always wanted to be.

But the leaf was not formed. Not more than a month went by in Denver before I was high again. Where had the willpower to turn down any offers gone? Within a week, there staggered the drunk kid again. It wasn't long before I eliminated school because I no longer cared about anything, including myself.

Back to Houston we went for the summer vacation. I straightened up to prove to all my friends how well I was doing. Once again, I thought I could do it all by myself, and once again, I was wrong. It took only a week before I was drunk. This drunk wasn't catastrophic. I wasn't injured for life, but, believe me, it was enough! It was enough for me to see that I couldn't control the drink, but rather, that it controlled me. The next day I talked to someone from the drug abuse program and she brought the facts home to me. I cried and felt suddenly helpless. I had to admit that I was powerless over intoxicants and that my life had become unmanageable.

After I had admitted this, I thought that my problems would wither and die, and that my new life would be a bed of roses. Well, it is, sort of, but I forgot about the ever-present thorns that go with beds of roses. Life seemed to be wonderful, for awhile, but I had real problems finding a power greater than myself. I didn't understand this "greater power," and because there was no gardener to tend my roses, the weeds were getting thick.

I spent weeks searching behind bushes, under trees, and just about everywhere for a Higher Power, but I found none. I expected a bolt of lightning or a burning bush and guess what? No go. I gave up my search and then it came. I don't care to say "God as we understand Him," but "God as we don't understand Him." I spent too much time trying to understand. The more I tried, the more human qualities I endowed Him with, for human qualities are what I comprehend. This was the problem. He is so powerful that I cannot understand Him, and He stays where he should, out of my reach. But when I endowed God with human qualities, I also had to give Him human frailties and thus brought Him down to my level, making Him a God I couldn't accept.

I returned to Denver for the school year, and quit attending A.A., and left it up to my Higher Power to keep me sober. His efforts, I thought, were all I needed. By November, I was in shreds and I started attending Alateen, even though someone had told me that what I really needed was to go to Alcoholics Anonymous. At Alateen we talked about A.A. a little bit, and I liked what I heard, but all the people in A.A. sounded like they would be so old. So I decided I would go to Alateen instead. I thought that talking with kids my own age would be all that I needed.

Alateen helped, for awhile, but eventually I found myself again hanging on by my fingernails. Out of desperation I called A.A. and asked about where I should go. Not more than five minutes later, a lady whom I will call Jan called me back. She picked me up that night and took me to an A.A. meeting. It seemed to me that several people in the meeting resented my being there because I was so young, and one man even confronted me, saying he had spilled more than I ever drank. I was stunned. But Jan told me not to let him bother me. Soon afterwards I learned to reply, "If you drank all you say you spilled, you would have gotten here as soon as I did too." or "What do you think I've been on, a picnic?"

A lot of good came out of that first night. Jan and I talked on the way home and we decided to start a teenage A.A. group. For many meetings she and I were sometimes the only ones present, and I relied on Jan for my sobriety for awhile. But I knew this could not last. Finally we got a place in a church to use for our meetings, and for months we stared at each other, and we talked, and we talked. Finally one night someone else showed up and from then on the group quickly grew. In fact, recently it has been crowded.

I grew right along with the group. I began working my steps more rigorously and have had many beautiful Twelfth Step calls. I found that the longer I was around A.A., the more acceptance I received from older people. I love young people's groups, but I have found that I need the regular meetings to make my program complete.

Over the few years I have been sober, I have learned about the thorns in my garden. One of the sharpest thorns was my social life. I wanted to make friends, but when it came to the usual crowds I found in school, I didn't really fit in. My life-style before I stopped drinking fit in with the revolutionaries and freaks and even though a lot of my thought patterns are still similar to theirs, they still get high, and that makes us very unlike. I never could relate to the jocks, and the really straight people drove me up a wall. After passing through many lonely days, I found a few friends, a few kids to spend my free time with. My true friends have come to me through A.A., and they are the ones I feel truly are what friends should be.

Although my problems still make me feel empty at times, the major gaps in my life have been filled. My Higher Power reveals things to me as I need them. He does give me what I need, just not always what I want. My story won't end until my life ends, and with the grace of God, I'll be smiling. The key to this program is honesty, open-mindedness, and willingness to change. Just because you are reading this book, I know you have a touch of each. Remember, the only requirement for membership in the program is a desire to live a life free from the bondage of drugs.

I am seventeen with three years sobriety and am not only free from the bondage of drugs, but am free from the bondage of self-centeredness. What I have found is a choice, a choice in everything that comes my way. I am no longer a prisoner of drugs and as the title says—I am young, sober and free. AND grateful!

2

We've All Been Hung Up On God

"To whom it may concern: HELP!"
Anonymous

Because of discouragements, because of failures, because of heart-aches, and because of those things that make you afraid, will you turn your back upon the opportunity before you now? The opportunity is to make your connection with the Powers of the Universe. You may decide not to—that is always one possible choice—but choosing to turn your back may be signing your own death warrant. We ask you to finish reading this chapter and then decide.

Now think. How could God, any God, will that any soul should perish? We believe that for every trial, every temptation, the Creative Forces of the Universe have provided a way out. And for us, it is this Program.

Before delving into the "God rap," it is important to speak of the spiritual foundation upon which our Program is based, without which our recovery would be improbable. Because of the three-fold nature of our disease, we see recovery as a three-fold process, the basis or foundation being spiritual. Recovery can be conceptualized like this:

Recovery on just one side of the triangle will not get us recovered, even a little bit. It's an all-the-way trip or it's no trip at all.

"But I've tried religion before," we can hear you saying, "and it never worked!" So have we. In fact most of us have tried several religions in all sincerity, striving to make the world come off good. It was not unusual to see us banging tamborines with the maharishis, on our knees in a cathedral, chanting with the Buddhists, or reading *The Prophet* on a mountaintop—*always* in an attempt to find the Answer. Through our past experiences, we have never found an Answer, as such, but forced by our experiences to look for help, we have discovered a way of life that works. To many of us, religion has represented a rigid dogma, but our spiritual Program represents a principled, loving way of life. And that difference is what we offer you. No dogma, no condemnation, just a simple, principled, loving way to live. And that brings us to the Second Step and the "God rap."

Step 2:   We came to believe that a power greater than ourselves could restore us to sanity.

The key to this whole process is willingness. Willingness to know about a Higher Power is all that is needed to start growing toward that knowledge. Some of us didn't have a problem believing. We believed all right, but God was obviously not interested in us because He hadn't worked in our lives. When we found ourselves in one or the other of these attitudes—either not believing or believing it wouldn't work—we prayed. When we start praying, just to pray for the willingness to believe (and believe it will work) is enough to add a new dimension in our lives. Don't let your own misunderstanding of God bind you to yourself and limit your ability to grow.

In order to maintain sobriety, it is an absolute necessity to seek a Power Source other than chemicals. You need a source that you can rely on. People who discover this Power Source agree that it is an inside job. Osmosis won't work; neither will another individual's concept of a Higher Power (HP) necessarily work for you for any length of time. In the beginning, you might try using your sponsor's HP. You might even use your home group as a Higher Power until you gain experience and knowledge for yourself. Oftentimes, in seeking God, we make our search more complicated (as we often do with other things) than necessary. When we go to meet God, we want—if not expect—claps of thunder, burning bushes, a divine telegram, or the God Experience to resemble the phantasmagoria of an acid trip. But almost always, the experience of the HP is more simple than that. One of our group describes his experience this way:

"I was bummed-out because I was trying to believe in God, praying like mad and nothing was happening to me; I couldn't feel anything. I told a priest friend of mine who was working with me about this and he said, 'You are sitting there waiting for a voice to come out of the corner. Well, just maybe instead of coming out of the corner, the voice is coming out of me.' From then on I knew God works through people, talks through people, and I was missing a lot because I was waiting for the voice from the corner. As time goes on, I see God all around me in people, places and things."

It is o.k. to be rational and hesitant—the only mistake you can make in the Second Step is to be unwilling.

Only a few words need to be written about the second half of the Second Step, "restore us to sanity." We don't claim insanity in a schizophrenic or psychotic sense of the medical profession. On the contrary, we are closer to the statement of Father Joe of the film *Chalk Talk* that the percentage of alcoholics who need psychiatric help is more than likely to be the same as for the rest of the population.

But let us refer to the mental obsession, the *insanity* of taking the first fix, pill, or drink. Why, after we have proven again and again that it doesn't work for us, do we continue to pop that pill, snort that coke, drink that wine? We call *that* insane. Our behavior, in that sense, *is* definitely unhealthy. However, it is only one symptom, and is not to be confused with the total disease. Remember, alcoholism, *is not* a symptom of mental illness; unhealthy thinking is often a symptom of alcoholism. And this brings us to Step Three.

Step 3: **We made a decision to turn our will and our lives over to the care of God *as we understood him.***

We assume that since you got this far, you can read. But if you're asking, "How can I turn my will and my life over to God?" then you can't read. We agree that you can turn your car keys (which you can see and touch) over to Mary (whom you can see and touch) but turning your will (that you can't see and touch) over to God (Whom you can't see and touch) would be impossible at this point. That's why you need to read the first four words, the magic words, "Made a decision to." We did not necessarily know *how* to make it. All we did was make a decision to do it, just as we all can make a decision to go to

India. We may not know how to go, whether by ship or plane, where to get the money, how to obtain visas and passports. But first, we make the decision and the execution of the decision comes later. This is our program: the decision first and the rest of the steps are the execution. If you decide you want to take the Third Step, you've already taken it.

Then comes another stumbling block. Many young people are afraid to make that decision, to let go of the reins. The fears come from many different points. "Maybe I'll never be able to have fun anymore," "I'm so young," "Probably I'll be singing hymns with A.A. and N.A. fanatics the rest of my life," "All the excitement of living will be gone," and, "I'll come off as a goody two-shoes," or just plain old fear of the unknown. We have all faced these fears, too. To put it bluntly, though, we had to grow up and be realistic. Fun and excitement? Upon closer examination we saw that throwing up, stumbling around, parents constantly screaming or punishing, car wrecks, screwed up boyfriend/girlfriend relationships, and being in constant terror of the cops did not exactly spell fun and excitement. Singing hymns with fanatics? That's a cop-out. We found joyful, laughing, growing kids and adults at our meetings. Coming off as a goody two-shoes? What's so great about coming off as a bad-ass?

What we're discussing here is our running our lives as opposed to letting God, as we understand Him, run our lives. Did our past really work out that well for us? Did the self-will, the insistence on doing-it-our-way approach to life work? Our efforts may or may not have been sincere, but always we found that WE were doing it—there was no place for God. We took the power to ourselves and that had been our prime mistake. We would like to note here that we do not consider ourselves weak people. Actually we are very strong people. We have to be to live for any length of time with this disease. But strength and power are not the same thing. They can be likened to heavy equipment and a driver. Construction equipment can tear down skyscrapers, lift tons of dirt. We've seen them do incredible things. The machines are strong, no doubt. But without the right driver, they can do tremendous damage, and without a driver who knew how to turn on the power, they can do nothing. We decided that our driving wasn't getting the job done, so we employed a new Driver and recognized that the power was not ours to claim. Even the breath we take at this very moment is not of our own power.

There is one more question we will ask of you who are still troubled with Step Three. If your way worked so well, why are you still searching for a way that works?

After all this explanation and exploration with you, we would like to drop to the basics of the first Three Steps. It *really* is a simple program but the simplicity escapes the complexity of our minds. The first Three Steps in simple form:

I can't;

He can;

I think I'll let Him.

We can analyze, rationalize, and intellectualize our way into or out of just about anything. So we ask you to stop the intellectual crap and just work the steps. Judge the results later; don't try to know the results first. You can't, you really can't. If we've learned nothing else we have learned this about life: You can analyze it to death.

Noel

Desperately, she sought to fill the
emptiness in herself.

Today I am looking at life the way it ought to be: good things are happening. The biggest change in my life today is an inside job, and the eyes I'm looking out of today see good things.

But it hasn't always been like this. Yeah, I remember what it was like before. I had one of those normal childhoods. You know the kind—full of loneliness, insecurity, remorse, fear, low self-esteem, and dishonesty. But I didn't have all those fancy words for it before. All I remember was that it felt BAD. No, I wasn't an orphan or a product of a broken home or a drunk at age three. Actually I don't know what it was that made me a drunk. But it happened. I became an alcoholic.

About seventeen years ago I was born in Africa. My dad was in the service at the time, and after a couple of years on that side of the world, my family moved to my dad's home town in Texas. Finally the time rolled around to where I can remember things: scraped knees and grandma and different houses and new friends. We moved around a lot. There was fear then about making new friends. "What do I say?" "How do I act?"

When school started it was even worse. I remember NOT KNOWING. I did not know the people around me, I did not know what to do so they'd like me, and I did not know what was wrong with me. I always had the feeling that I was not quite as good as they were. I would see people around me and they were so smart. All the girls who wore pretty flowered dresses made me jealous. Those girls seemed to be able to talk to the boys and I couldn't. Everyone around seemed to have friends but me. The answer to that? Well, we moved again, and, for a while, I figured that would be an answer because it got me off the hook. I never stayed and worked anything out or learned to face a problem. Wonderful! Now I got to start all over. Brand new fear, insecurity, and loneliness. Or should I say, "brand new BAD."

Well, I went through third and fourth grade. Those weren't my favorite years. More then ever before I felt left out. There was a clique I looked up to so much, but they looked down on me. The girls would never talk to me; the boys seldom did either. Near the end of the fourth grade, the most popular boy in the class had a party, and everyone was invited. Even me.

I recall sitting on the porch and slowly, slowly all the kids went around to the side of the house. Finally, one other girl and I were left. The vague idea that the other kids were playing kissy-kissy or God knows what was in my head. Then two boys walked up to us. One boy said to the other, "She's cute, let's get her." And they took the other girl off to the side, too. I sat there on the porch, alone, eating my cupcake. I remember that it didn't feel too good on the inside. I began to hate those people then, but still I wanted them to like me. And then it was moving time again.

I changed schools. Of course, here again I found another set of people I wanted. If these people would only like me, everything would be o.k. And, lo and behold, I discovered something that worked. It was called dishonesty. I could lie myself into being whatever I wanted to be. I could be popular. I could have boyfriends. I could be happy. I began to invent people and tell my friends about them—from fifth to eighth grade this was what I did. My fear and insecurity were covered up by lying. All I wanted was acceptance and love. Because I was incapable of giving it to myself, I sought it from others. If they thought I was o.k., I would be o.k. Then and only then. This meant I had to do what they did, such as smoking cigarettes and stealing and drinking. I also had a feeling that my friends got high. Since I wanted what they had, I felt I had to follow. At school I would see the people that seemed to have something special. They wore faded, ragged, old blue jeans and had an empty look in their eyes. They were unafraid. No one could tell them what to do. I *wanted* that. I would hear them giggling and talking about marijuana and quaaludes and how blown they'd gotten the night before. And I wanted that, too.

At our family get-togethers there would usually be lots of liquor. I remember I would always sneak a little behind their backs, although I'm not sure why, but never enough to get tipsy. Somehow, I knew that the secret to being happy was hidden inside that bottle. Later I would tell my friends about how much I drank; a little lying would make me o.k. I just wanted to be loved. This search for approval didn't always lead me astray; in one way, it helped.

In the city where I lived there was an organization much like A.A.—the Palmer Drug Abuse Program—except that most of the people in it were from ages 13 to 25. I had heard about it and one day, with a couple of my friends who were having trouble with dope, I went to a meeting. I told myself, "I'm doing this for my friends." Although I just came along for the ride, I found something there I had never found before. Here was a group of people who seemed to be happy and didn't even get high. I couldn't believe it. They had a loving, fantastic fellowship, and, of course, I wanted to be a part of it. They said it was simple: just make meetings, stay sober, and follow these Twelve Steps. That was easy. I had nothing else to do, so why not make meetings. Even though I drank, I never got high, so staying clean did not present a problem.

However, the part about the Twelve Steps was something else. Hell, I didn't have a problem, why should I follow these steps? They said the answers to all my troubles were there, that's why. Fine, o.k. So for the next six months I stuck with this program, stayed sober, and followed the Third Step—a little. Most of the Steps I followed by picking and choosing. I eliminated Step One, the Fifth Step inventory, and whatever else seemed uncomfortable. After all, I had complete control of my life.

With this attitude, I made little progress, and that only because I got honest with my friends. I told them that all the people I told them about before did not exist. They were not there. Ah, relief. No more "ducking and dodging." When I got honest, a big hunk of fear and insecurity was removed, but I still had this big hole inside of me that needed to be filled. For some reason I chose not to fill it—I hadn't gotten the message!

After all this time of sticking around and staying straight, I still wanted to get high. "I could," I conned myself, "I was in control." Little by little, I stopped hanging around people in the Program and started to run around with people who got high. And sure enough, it was only a matter of time till I got high.

I won't forget when it started. I went out with some people and all I was going to do was drink half a beer. Just one-half. Certainly that wasn't a slip. Some rationalization! After I drank it, I wasn't so sure. Of course I wasn't drunk, but something happened to my thinking. I figured, "Well, hell, I've blown it. Now I might as well get good and loaded." Which I proceeded to do. My "friends" were very nice about us all smoking some pot, and they even bought more booze because I wasn't as high as I wanted to be. In fact, for the next six months, I was never as high as I wanted to be.

The details of the next half-year are not important. All that is important is that I spent a lot of time and energy trying to fill the hole inside that refused to be filled. I was sure that the secret still was inside of that bottle but I could never find it. Bottle after bottle was poured into that hole deep inside me, never filling it, never patching me up. When the people around me said, "O.k., I'm high. I don't want anymore," I wanted more. All my actions centered around one objective: getting loaded.

For most of this time I was still on the fringes of the Program. Often I would go and find some other fellow losers and brag about how recently I'd gotten loaded. It was insane, "I've got less sobriety than you!" Bragging about negative things didn't fill my emptiness either. And the damn hole just got deeper and deeper.

There were a few sober intervals when I found a happiness that I had never had before, but again I would blow it and get loaded. *I could not stop.* I needed a power greater than myself—something obvious to everyone but me. I would make a decision that I was going to get back in the Program for good, but that old will power just wouldn't work, and I got high again.

Misery surrounded me. I could not understand why nothing worked. Finally, when I had about half-a-day's dryness, I went to a meeting, a special, twenty-four-hour-long meeting. Everyone around me laughed and had fun. They felt loved and serene and I felt one inch tall. I went through that entire meeting feeling BAD. The hole inside was still there. I could not understand why everyone around me was happy and I wasn't. Maybe they had something I didn't.

A couple of days later something happened. I am not sure why it happened then and not before, but I am sure it was a gift from God. That day I got sick and tired of being sick and tired. I did not want that feeling anymore. The people with the faded blue jeans and the empty look had nothing to offer me anymore. I *had* to make a decision, and it was that the program and sobriety were the only way. For the first time in my life, I was willing to do anything to stay sober, and I knew I could't do it by myself. I had to have a Higher Power.

With my back up against a wall, I gave up. Finally I said it and meant it: "I can't, He can, I think I'll let Him." The fight was over, the struggle gone and that felt GOOD. At this point I had made the most important discovery of my life. The result was that the hole inside me was getting patched. Where the booze had poured right through that emptiness, love, sharing, and caring started to stick around the edges. The more I got, the more that stuck, until finally the hole was filled.

For the next two and one-half years, good replaced bad, openness replaced mad, happy replaced sad. The Twelve Steps have been my path to completeness. There stll are hard times because growing is usually painful, but I'm neither alone nor empty. We do this together. ALL our steps say WE, not I.

The things I have learned are indescribable, but let me mention a few:

- Today I can love myself AND others
- I *deserve* to stay clean and sober
- I know everything is going to be o.k. I've gained serenity
- God is in control. I don't have to carry that burden any longer
- I can give what I have been given so freely—experience, strength, and hope
- When I think things cannot get any better, they often do
- People love me. I am not alone.

These things are available to all of us. I know that my completeness can be your completeness, too. We are here, hoping for you, praying that you find some of what we have, and we will help you patch your soul, repairing all the holes in your life.

3

Escape To Reality

"You can climb out of your bottle or fit or bag and notice that the world isn't really worth hiding from."

Jimi

It is now time to study and apply ourselves. It is time to come out of the fog of the past, clear the garbage from our minds, and learn to deal with the world from a free mind rather than a drug-soaked brain. Once you have examined and taken the first Three Steps, you have passed through the acceptance part of the program and now will begin the action part of the program, Steps Four through Nine. You should take the time to first read the main texts of A.A. and N.A., as they contain the heart of our recovery program. These books would include *Alcoholics Anonymous*—called "The Big Book" by a lot of people—*Twelve Steps and Twelve Traditions of A.A.*, and the *Twelve Steps and Twelve Traditions of N.A.* What we are setting down here is only meant as a supplement to draw you closer to the group to which you belong, and to give you some insights by way of the experiences we have had as members of Alcoholics Anonymous and Narcotics Anonymous. Hearing each other's story helps each of us.

Some of the most important years of our lives were spent in the ozone. We missed a lot of our natural growing up processes or we experienced them behind a screen of mind-affecting chemicals. So actually we did not grow up naturally and this has caused stupidly naive or even "bent" personalities. Without the escape of drugs, we must now deal with life at a more rapid pace, at a later age. Yet we do have a choice about dealing with life: either we deal with life or we get stoned. Nobody says it's going to be easy. But dealing with life *is* simple and can be done, providing we don't procrastinate or rationalize our way out of it. To do either or both of those would make a joke out of the first

Three Steps, and, in fact, would neutralize any benefits we might expect from a sober life.

Many benefits explode once we start performing Step Four.

Step 4: We made a searching and fearless moral inventory of ourselves.

Anybody who has ever worked in a retail store or a grocery for any length of time knows what an inventory is without being told. An inventory is really just a matter of counting up the particular things you have on hand and making out a list. For us in A.A. or N.A., taking an inventory of ourselves does *not* have to be a big deal.

What we want to do is look at our behavior for things that we think we did that were wrong. The point isn't to make us look as bad as we feel. We take this inventory just to really see what we have to deal with in our lives. Most of us, in fact, tended to make ourselves look a little—or a lot—worse than we really were. How does Step Four work? Simple. You insert pencil in hand, apply it to paper in front of you and write. Yeah, it's really that simple and any number of brilliant "Yes, buts ..." will not impress us as our "Yes, buts ..." did not impress the older members of the Fellowships as they walked us through the Steps. So get to work.

Although there is a full explanation of the inventory in the book *Alcoholics Anonymous* (*Cf.* p. 65), we offer the following chart as a further guide because we did not always identify with some of the Fourth Step examples shown to us by older members. If we wanted to look at our resentments, our inventories would look like this:

INVENTORY

Person, place thing or idea	Why resented	What I thought and how I felt	Character defect revealed
Sue	Laughing at me	I think she is laughing at me sexually humiliated	Poor self-image; sexual insecurity
Joe	Acts tough; Acts superior	I want to impress my friends but scared	poor self-image; false pride; fear
Self	I let Joe do this	I cut him down; angry	dishonesty; maliciousness
Teacher	Caught me cheating on exam	I had every right; it's a stupid class to take out time for study; self-justified; embarrassed	dishonesty with self; dishonesty with others; irresponsibility; untrustworthiness; false pride
Father	criticizes me for joining A.A.	He's a hypocrite for judging me when he has a possible drinking problem of his own; hurt, unsure, angry	narrow-mindedness; non-sympathetic; self-centeredness; insecurity
My face	pimples	I blame my mom for serving greasy food; angry; self-conscious	false pride; displaced emotions; dishonesty
Myths around masturbation	Made me feel abnormal	I pretended I was "normal"; guilty	dishonesty; false pride; sexual insecurity; fear

Then we do the same kind of chart on the other things we feel were wrong. You don't have to worry about getting every example. All you need to do, really, is to be honest and not try to avoid any behavior that you thought might be wrong. Honesty is what is important.

We have to stress that being honest to the best of our ability in Step Four leads us to an honest Step Five. By the time we finish doing Step Four, most of our self-centeredness should be staring us in the face. Boy, had we really thought a lot about our impact on society. Somehow we had felt we were *so* unique, *so* different, or *so* special. But it took only a little honesty to admit that the universe would run quite well without us. One of our group described her progress through Steps Four and Five this way:

> "When it came time for me to take my Fourth and Fifth Steps, I feared being honest. Some of the things I had done seemed so bad to me that if anyone found out about them, I was afraid that I would be locked up. I was sure that people would never talk to me again. So it was a shock to find the person I took the Step with had done many of the same things I did and *more*. We aren't so horrible as we may have thought. It is such a relief to know that we aren't so special. Thinking about it beforehand, I almost got drunk, but learning I was not alone took a load off my back."

Step 5:   We admitted to God, to ourselves, and to another human being the exact nature of our wrongs.

It's seldom a negative experience to take the Fifth Step. In fact, most of us felt a tremendous sense of relief, a burden lifted from our shoulders. It was great! However, let us caution you—please take this step with someone you trust and who is unlikely to be hurt by all the things you say. We know your parents love you and at times you must feel really close, but doing a Fifth Step with them should be carefully considered. Is there anything that will hurt them? Might they, in fits of anger, use something against you? The same goes for girlfriends and boyfriends. Are you sharing too much for them to handle? The best seems to be a clergy person specially trained for this step. A *trusted* close friend or an older member on the program who is *not* too close to your parents might be wise. On this step the caution lights are flashing yellow.

Step 6:   We were entirely ready to have God remove all these defects of character.

As in Step Three, the key here is willingness. Are we willing to have our faults (sometimes seen as mountains) removed? Praying for willingness now is a start, but it isn't enough. We have to perform some actions. First of all we show our willingness in Step Six by stopping any behavior connected to our character defects. If, for instance, we have identified revenge as a defect, then the next time we want to take revenge on someone, we simply stop the action of trying to get revenge. Do not tell his parents, turn her in, or poison their cat. How can we truly say we are willing to have our faults removed if we follow through on these inclinations to get even. Stopping the revenge-behavior is true willingness. The defect may still be there, eating us up, but we act willing and then we go on to Step Seven.

Step 7:   We humbly asked Him to remove our shortcomings.

Wow! These shortcomings have been constant close companions for years; they're comfortable and "easy" for us, a whole lot easier, it seems, than a way of life about which we have little concept. Actually this is not so, but when one is in error and practices that error, the error becomes more and more prominent in one's life, natural to think, and easy to practice. Applying new principles appears difficult at first. We no longer can use our defects as an excuse for self-will trips saying such things as, "Well, what do you expect, I'm sick." or "Sorry, I've always had a problem with gossip." Nobody really cares if you're sick or have a problem with gossip. They don't want you shitting on them anymore, and in reality, if you tread on others, you're treading on yourself. So we think the easier way, the more workable way, is to let go of the defects. If you maintain honesty, your Higher Power will reveal to you what you need to know, when you need to know it, and remove it when you are ready and willing to ask.

Step 8:   We made a list of all persons we had harmed, and became willing to make amends to them all.

Most of this list can be written by referring back to the Fourth Step. It is important, however, not to justify our own behavior and conveniently leave names off the list. It doesn't matter if Jane Doe took your boyfriend away, that's no excuse for telling one little lie about her. If we harmed her, we harmed her, and her name goes on the list. When the list is completed, we affirm our willingness, then we go immediately to Step Nine.

Step 9:   We made direct amends to such people wherever possible, except when to do so would injure them or others.

Here we meet the hang-ups of the past as we would have others meet us with their wrong-doings. Did we steal money? It needs to be paid back, even if it takes years to pay it all. Did we gossip, tell lies? They need to be undone, regardless of our image. All we have to do—and it is a lot—is to admit that what we said wasn't true. But we don't find it necessary to plunge into lengthy explanations or cornball confessions. Just open, direct admission of wrongs and what we intend to do about it is sufficient. We find that many of our amends are made, for example, to our parents, or the school system, by living this new way of life. We don't limit ourselves to saying, "Sorry, Mom, that I was such a screw-up." We *show* her we are changing, and that is living through an amend.

In our zest for progress, we oftentimes unthinkingly involve or incriminate others so that they are harmed. It is recommended to THINK and ask for guidance before making amends all over the countryside. We should admit *our* wrongdoings; not the wrongdoings of other people. This is a good time to go to your sponsor and have a thorough discussion about these matters. Don't incriminate friends or strangers from your dope-dealing days and don't "confess" things to your family that may cut them to the core. They have hurt enough while watching your disease progress, and they shouldn't have to hurt now while watching your recovery come about.

Once the past is cleared, our fears of the future begin disappearing. Living in the here-and-now proves to be an exciting, challenging path to follow. After all, today is all we can ever experience at any given time. We are no longer bummed out by the there and then or overwhelmed by the where and when. Our path represents a part of a process and we begin to see rhyme and reason, and even gain trust in the process. We begin to feel like living and become a part of the great flow of life. Some of us even find ourselves eventually saying things like, "I'm a grateful alcoholic and addict," when gratitude for this disease was an idea that had totally confused us before.

In the light of our expanding consciousness it dawns on us that life is a very happy and secure reality.

Lee

*His conversations with other people were
mostly interruptions with his inner dialogue.*

"Oscar Lee—Oscar Lee—Get up and get in the kindling and coal. You
didn't do it last night so get up and go do it and hurry up. You never do anything
you're supposed to and ...."

THUT!

*"O.k.! O.k.! God damn, you don't have to throw a butcher knife. That stuck
in my pillow! You're crazy!"*

"Don't you talk to me that way! You know better than that—After all I've
done for you! You smart alec! Get out there and get that kindling and don't
you talk back to me! I'll get that razor strap."

*Crack! Crack! That's Grandma's neck. Whap! Whap! That's
her arms. Thud! That's her old wrinkled face. Crack! That's her
back .... I hate her! I hate her! I'm going to run away!*

"Oscar Lee. You got that kindling? Bring it in here and quit messing
around. You think I got all day? Listen, mister, if I hated someone as much as
you hate me I wouldn't live in the same house with them. And don't you try to
leave either. If I ever see you going down that lane to the highway like you're
leaving, I'll shoot you right in the back! I sure will. Don't you ever try to run
away. Now you get out there and feed and water those rabbits—and don't
you forget any, either. You left a cage open yesterday, and that old brown doe
got away and that old rusty dog had to catch her. Now, you mind what I tell
you! You never do anything right nohow ...."

*God damn rabbits—God damn Grandma—God damn every-
thing!*

THAT WAS MY CHILDHOOD. GRANDMA ... DAD ... PATTY ... WHO THE HELL WAS TO BLAME FOR ME BEING SO SCREWED UP? NOBODY WANTED ME. NOBODY EVER DID AND HIGH SCHOOL WAS NO EXCEPTION.

*   *   *

"Oscar, I hope we're not going to have any problems here. We have your records from Grand Junction Jr. High and I guess that's enough said about that."

"Ya, o.k. I'll try to keep my nose clean."

"We're going to take you around and introduce you to your teachers and show you your locker and explain the rules of Central High School. We expect ...."

I wonder when he's gonna shut up and let me go.

"Mr. Miller, this is a new student, a transfer from Grand Junction—Lee, this is Mr. Miller your World History teacher ..."

My God! Those are beautiful eyes! I wonder if she'll like me—I hope I get to sit next to her. What a gorgeous chick!

"Uh, ya, Mr. Miller, umh?"

Why do I feel so weak and confused?

*   *   *

"Lee, what makes you think you can walk out of here, be gone for three weeks and stroll back in as if nothing had happened?"

Oh boy, big deal!

"Mister, you have one more chance in school—That's because your sister went before the School Board and really stuck her neck out for you. One step out of line and you're out for good. Do you hear me?"

"Yes, sir, I'll be good!"

How many times have I heard this crap, "One more chance?" I'm sick of it! "This is your last chance."—bullshit!

"Yes, sir, I hear you. I'll be good."

* * *

It was Marylins' mother. She transferred Marylin to Grand Junction so she wouldn't be around me. Why can't people just stay out of my life —leave me alone?

"Marylin, I guess this is goodbye. I have another girl pregnant, and I guess I'm gonna have to marry her—I guess it don't matter anyway. You're going with someone else. I love you—"

"Lee, I think I know how to solve this. You wouldn't have to marry her if you were already married to someone else—ME."

"Do you mean it? Would you marry me? God, I'd do anything if you would!"

* * *

"Hey, Lee, don't hog that hooch! Someone else might want some of it. Hand it back up here or I'll kick your ass."

"You and who's army?"

Betty's pregnant, I'm kicked out of the house, no job and Marylin don't love me. Running away with some guy for three days to Utah—I don't want her back—I want her dead! I want me dead. Why was I ever born, anyway. To hell with it.

"Hand that bottle back here. Don't you think anybody else gets thirsty?"

* * *

I NEVER THOUGHT I'D GET THROUGH HIGH SCHOOL AND LOOKING BACK ON THE TIME RIGHT AFTER HIGH SCHOOL, I ALMOST WISHED I HADN'T.

* * *

God damn! Three-and-a-half years in the army, getting discharged in New York, waking up in Washington D.C., thinking I was in Chicago— finding a job, a rooming house room, I haven't touched a girl in months —Where the hell is it all heading? The queers, the whores, the hell! I'm twenty years old and I've been a million miles and I still feel like I'm fourteen! I wish I had a woman—any God damn woman. I should have married that girl in Germany. What was her name .... I'm gonna go have a beer. I should get cleaned up. I'll just have a couple and then I'll get cleaned up and go out for dinner.

"Gimme a shot 'n' a beer."

I'll get cleaned up and go to a nice restaurant and I'll meet a really nice chick—a lean lanky blonde with really big tits and nice clothes. She'll be really nice to me and I'll take her home to her apartment and it'll be all real feminine and we'll talk and have another drink and dance and then we'll go to bed ....

"Another one."

If I had a model 'A' with a Chrysler 300 and dual carburetors and a four speed and dual glass packs, I'd be running a hundred miles an hour and playing the radio full blast and passing everything on the road and I'd come over a hill and there'd be Marylin and a girl friend in her mother's old Merc and I'd be going so fast, all they'd see is a streak going past. But Marylin would think she recognized me and they'd speed up to try to catch me and ....

"Another one."

If that big guy came over here and said something to me I'd say "Why don't you sit down and shut up," and he'd take a swing at me and I'd throw up my left arm to block the blow and I'd grab him by the front of his shirt and I'd throw him over my right hip and he'd crash into the juke box. He'd get up and I'd grab him by the ears and as I pulled his head down I would slam my knee up into his face—then I'd kick him in the nuts and as he doubled up I'd slam a hard right into his left ear and he'd go down like a ton of bricks and I'd just walk back to the bar and finish my beer and casually walk out the back door before the cops came.

"Yeah, the same."

I'm really a lot different person than anyone knows—I'm smarter and tougher and I can draw and nobody knows any of that. Nobody really knows me at all. They think I'm just a tramp and a coward. They should get to know me. I've just had bad luck and I never really ever had a chance. Grandma messed up my life and I don't have a chance. If I had a chance, I'd show 'em.

"Yeah, one more."

I really have good thoughts when I'm drinking but I can't ever remember them the next morning. I should write 'em down at night. Then the next morning I could read 'em and remember 'em and then people would know that I'm not what they think I am 'cause then they'd know 'cause I'd know . . . .

"O.k., o.k., I'm leaving anyway."

Now where do I wanna go? I need a girl—I'm gonna hide in this alley and if a woman comes by I'm gonna grab her and pull her into the alley and make her have sex with me, but I'm not gonna hurt her—I want her to like me—I want her to want me—Ummmm if she had long hair and nice legs and boobs and was wearing pink lipstick and put her arms around my neck and pulled her dress up and oh . . . oh . . . oh . . . . I'm gonna go to that coffee shop down the street.

"Just coffee, black."

I gotta get home—I gotta get up in three hours.
Where's that key? I know I had it . . . . I can't find it, this is my door. I'll just go to the bathroom. I might as well sleep in the tub.
Wha' th' hell! What 'm I doin in this water? I'm all wet—It's morning. I gotta get to work. I gotta get out of these wet clothes —I'll get fired—
My God! Gotta get some coffee! Gotta get something on my stomach. Gotta have a cigarette! Wonder if anyone saw me sleeping in the tub with my clothes on. Did I turn on the water, who did? Wher'd I go last nite? What happened? Gotta get to work—Gonna get fired.

"Sorry I'm late—I didn't have bus fare. I had to walk."

"What's that stuck in your eyebrows?"

"I don't know."

> *My God, it's puke. I got sick last nite in that tub.*

"Go and get us some coffee and when you get back, I've got some errands for you."

"Anybody else want coffee?"

> *I'm never gonna drink again! I think I'm gonna die. If that black girl in the delicatessen would be nice to me I'd marry her. I wouldn't care what anybody said. I'd hate to meet her family though—and everytime we went somewhere I'd have to fight some big black dude—I couldn't do it. I wonder what chiggers are—she said she had chigger bites. Are they like my cock roaches? Only they bite. I guess that's what they are —at least I'd like to get in her pants. I wonder if she'd go out with me. Where would I take her?*
>
> *What a day. I gotta catch the boss before he leaves and get some money.*

"Mr. B., I need a couple bucks. Can I get enough for supper and breakfast and bus fare?"

"Why are you always broke the next day after pay day every week? You should budget your money. I'll make you a deal. If you'll come to work on time every day for five days in a row, I'll give you a nickel raise and everytime you do that, I'll give you another nickel raise until you're making so much I can't afford to pay you and then I'll go to work for you. I may as well. My kids don't want anything to do with this business. It embarrasses them. Here's five dollars. Don't spend it all in one place."

"Thanks boss, I'll see you in the morning, a quarter to nine. I promise."

> *I'm not gonna get drunk tonight. I'll just have a couple beers and go do my laundry.*

"A shot 'n' a beer."

*   *   *

LIFE WENT ON.

*   *   *

"Alright pal, into the wagon. You're going downtown."

"What the hell! Alright everyone sit down and shut up—you! Leave him alone ...."

What in hell's goin' on? Is that a guy or a girl? That's a man in a dress. Oh my God! What am I doin' here? What am I in for? How long will I be here? What did I do?

"Oscar L. B.?"

"Yeah, that's me."

"Do you want to do something about your drinking problem?"

"I don't have a drinking problem."

"Do you want to get out of trouble?"

"Yeah."

What am I in here for? I need a cigarette. How long will I be here? What did I do? Am I gonna get killed? God, these are terrible people! God, if you'll get me out of here, I'll quit drinking. I'll quit smoking, playing with myself, I'll quit cussing, I'll do anything! Please God!

"You wanna give blood for cigarettes? You can get a carton of cigarettes for a pint of blood."

"O.k."

My God, two packs in each end and a two-by-four in the middle. I wonder who did that? Oh well.

"Hey pal, gimme smoke."

"Yeah, me too."

"Give me one."

"O.k."

Shit!

"We're gonna see a movie today and I want you animals to act like people."

"I want all blacks to sit on the left side and whites on the right and I don't want no trouble!"

> *Christ, there's at least two hundred of them and one, two, three— shit, fourteen of us. Why is he doing this? Those guys are standing up along the wall and sitting in the aisle and our side is empty! He's trying to start a race riot! Well, I'm not going to sleep tonight anyway.*

"Oscar L. B., you're charged with being drunk and disorderly and resisting arrest—How do you plead?"

"Guilty, Your Honor."

"The man ahead of you has been in this jail over forty times and the man behind you over ninety times. From the condition you were in when you came in, I have no reason to believe you won't be back. To keep from having to sentence you then, I'll just sentence you now. I sentence you to life on the installment plan. You can serve it any way you like, ten, thirty, ninety days at a time or in larger quantities. There is an alternative—if you're interested, go through the door in the back of the court room."

"God grant me the serenity to accept the things I cannot change, the courage to change the things I can, and the wisdom to know the difference. Hi, I'm Bill, and I'm an alcoholic. I come down here every morning to repay the debt to the man that helped me when I got out. Alcoholics Anonymous can show you a way of life that can make it possible for you to live without liquor and jails. If you want what we have and are willing to go to any lengths to get it, it works."

> *Man, does that air smell good. Green grass! Trees! Birds! I didn't know there were birds in Washington, D.C. God, it's good to be alive! I never felt so good. Four days behind bars can give a man a different outlook. I'll never go back there. No more booze! I'll go to their meetings and live up to the conditions of the probation. I don't ever want to go back there.*

*   *   *

Got my job back, a place to live and everything's o.k. All I need is a car and a girl!

*   *   *

ALTHOUGH I STILL HAD SOME MORE DRINKING TO DO, IT WASN'T LONG BEFORE I FINALLY ARRIVED BACK AT THE DOORS OF A.A. I WAS TWENTY-TWO.

*   *   *

Wha' th' hell! Where am I? What's goin' on?

"... so I went to A.A. and I haven't had a drink since."

I'm in an A.A. meeting! How'd I get here? Oh, my head! I wonder who sent me—Where have I been? What have I done?

"Oh no, I don't have anything to say."

I don't want to drink. I want to work and get rich and fall in love. Maybe I can get Marylin back, or maybe I can fall in love with some farm girl and have a nice house. Maybe she'll be really pretty and really love me exactly like I am . . . . Or maybe I can put on some weight, build up some muscles and make a lot of money. Maybe I can get a truck and haul over the road and have lots of waitresses or maybe I can be a famous commercial artist and have a pretty secretary that would fall in love with me. Ah, what the hell. I'm not ever gonna be anything!

*   *   *

Why can't I be like other people? Why am I so strange? Other people just go along doing whatever they do and I walk around crazy. Pat and Roy would have sent me to college as long as I wanted to go. Dad and I could have made it if he wasn't so much like Grandma. Why couldn't Marylin love me like I love her? What am I gonna do?

*   *   *

I'm in a liquor store! How the hell did I get here? I don't remember walking here. I don't want to drink!

"Uh, I'll just have a pack of Pall Malls."

Better get to the club, maybe Abe'll be there!

* * *

"Abe, I just found myself in a liquor store and I don't remember the last several blocks I walked before I got there. I'm scared. I just got a pack of cigarettes and got my butt down here. Have you ever heard of anybody doin' that?"

"Not that, exactly, but I have heard of people having delayed reactions to alcohol and that could be what it was. You're going to need God's help if you're gonna stay sober."

"Abe, I don't know how to pray. I'm not sure I believe in God. Maybe good —but I don't know about God!"

"I didn't either, I just talked to him like I do to you and slowly I started getting answers and I have come to rely on Him over the years."

God, whoever You are—whatever You are—if you exist—I need help!

"Lee, I've known you for almost a year now, and I think we're pretty good friends. Being blind, I can't tell how old you are. You must be about my age from your story. I'm fifty one."

"No, Abe, I'm only twenty-three. I've just got a lot of miles . . . ."

Does he know I've been lying? Does he know what I'm really like? Would he still like me if he really knew?

* * *

EVEN THOUGH I HAD TO CONSIDER MYSELF AS ONE OF THOSE THAT WAS SICKER THAN OTHERS, I TRUDGED THE ROAD OF HAPPY DESTINY, AND MINGLED WITH MY MANIA WERE MANY HAPPY TIMES.

* * *

I don't think this is gonna get it. This is the fourth time I've been in group therapy. The first time was when I was sober twenty-two months and everything turned to shit and I wanted to drink. Then when my first wife and I split up. Then that time I was going to slit my throat when I couldn't decide whether I was gay, straight, both, neither. Now another love affair down the tube and married on the rebound and to someone I don't even like. Why don't I just walk out on the whole thing and go find Marylin. Maybe I was so screwed up when I was in Chicago, I just imagined that she was a lesbian. God knows I've imagined an awful lot of things. I don't know what to believe. Well, I can believe some things—A.A. has helped me stay sober. I couldn't do that on my own. I am sure that I want to make my living in art—well—signs are close enough for now, anyway. I don't think therapy is the answer. It's a good thing I can go to the club and release all my frustrations.

"Hi, Henrietta, whendja get outta jail?"

"Hi, you rotten kid. Why don't you go back home?"

"I don't have a home. You gonna let me move in with you?"

"Not on your life!"

"If you're not nice to me I'm gonna throw your coat in the trash again."

"You're gonna pay the cleaning bill this time, too."

"Good morning, Bill. Sausage 'n' eggs and a bowl of snot!"

"You really know how to improve everyone's appetite, don't you? Why don't you eat at home and let everyone else enjoy eating here?"

"I'm just trying to spread joy and love."

"Why don't you wash your hair?"

"You just wish you had some!"

"Oh, you're rotten!"

"Thank you."

"I thought you were going to Phoenix."

"I was, but I couldn't afford to go to Castle Rock."

"Isn't your business doing any good?"

"Naw, I'm no business man. I'm a pretty decent sign painter, but I'm a terrible manager. I just don't seem to be able to keep it together. I make a bundle one week and nothing the next, and I don't manage money any better then I manage business."

"If I had your talent I'd be a millionaire."

"Yeah, and if I could hang on to money the way you do, I'd own Denver."

"Lee, your breakfast is up."

"O.k. Thanks Bill. That looks almost good enough to eat! Hi Russ, where ya been, in jail?"

"No, I have to stay out so I can pay your bail."

"How's your wife and my kids?"

"You want 'em back?"

"No thanks, I can't handle the ones I got."

"Thought you were going to Phoenix."

"I ran out of money before I got out of town."

"Aren't you going?"

"No, I don't think so. I talked to some people that I've known for a long time. They could see through it, and see the same old pattern that I've repeated so many times before."

"What are you gonna do? Just keep screwing up like you have been?"

"I imagine! No, I hope not. I'm just gonna start the Program over again. Christ! How many times I've done that! Four trips to the funny farm, and all that crap. You'd think I could get a handle on the thing."

"Lee, you haven't had a drink in what, five years? That's something! Be a little easier on yourself!"

"Sometimes I think I'm too easy on me. What's it gonna take to get me going?"

"Maybe you need a vacation. Just go off by yourself for a week or so and go fishing or something. How long has it been since you took a day off?"

"I don't know, several weeks. Well, I gotta go."

I wonder if I should check into Fort Logan again. I don't know after four trips through there and then a year and a half on the staff, I wonder if it'd do any good. NO—I'm just gonna start over again in the Program and get with the people. I wish I had some answers!

*   *   *

EVERY MORNING I PRAYED.

*   *   *

God, I'm powerless over alcohol and my life is unmanageable. You can restore me to sanity and today I'm going to let You. Please direct my thinking today, especially that it be divorced from self-pity, dishonest, self-seeking motives, jealousy or lust. I offer myself to You to build with me and to do with me as You will. Relieve me from the bondage of self that I may better do Your will. Take my difficulties that victory over them may bear witness to those I would help of Your power, Your love, and Your way of life. Please help me stay sober today and show me how I can help a suffering alcoholic.

*   *   *

THERE WERE UPS AND DOWNS, BUT ALWAYS, IF I WAS WILLING, PEOPLE IN THE FELLOWSHIP TOOK CARE OF ME.

*   *   *

"Frank, John, Dave—I'm leaving town. I've made up my mind to go to Arizona to see a girl that I've known for eighteen years. I've already told Kathy and Jimi. Course, Kathy doesn't think it's too good an idea, but Jimi thought it was great. I'm going to build that car—boat—plane, or at least a scale model of it and try to market that. I've made up my mind and all I need is enough

money to give Kathy a little and have enough left to get out of town. I can work my way to Phoenix painting signs.''

I don't seem to be making it here. I can't seem to keep my business together. I can't keep a job—I can't keep myself in love with my wife and kids. I can't seem to work the Program well enough to get my head straight. I need to go away and do what I want to and see if I can become what I think I can.

''Lee, can you get to Phoenix sober?''

''I think so. I don't know.''

''You seem pretty tired. You sure you should leave in that condition? I think you're where I was a couple months ago. I got to the point where I couldn't work, I couldn't play. I couldn't seem to make myself do anything. I was exhausted, mentally, physically, and spiritually. I finally just came to a stand still and just sat in one spot and recovered.''

''Frank, that sounds just like where I'm at.''

''You don't have the power to go to Arizona. You are in trouble and you need to just stand still and try to start your Program over again, as if you didn't have ten years. If you can be as open as you can and don't run, you have a chance. If you run now, I think you'll be drunk very shortly.''

''Get with your people that you've known a long time, the ones you're close to and try to start over. You're probably in a pretty good place if you can do that. You may be right on the brink of a break down.''

''O.k., I'll just not make a decision—for now. I'll just decide not to leave yet and see where that takes me—Thanks fellows, I guess I really needed this meeting more than I knew ....''

* * *

TODAY

* * *

God, I'm powerless over alcohol and my life is unmanageable. You can restore me to sanity and today I'm gonna let You. Please direct my thinking today especially that it be divorced from self-

pity, dishonest, self-seeking motives, jealousy, and lust. You know, God, the jealousy is gone. I don't know what You're doing with the lust but that's Your business. I guess I could be a little more co-operative by not buying the dirty books and stuff like that. I offer myself to you to build with me and to do with me as You will. Relieve me from the bondage of self that I may better do Your will. I guess You have done that. I seem to be effective in helping other people and I seem to add some happiness to other people's lives. I know I make a lot of people laugh and some really like to see me. Take away my difficulties that victory over them may bear witness to those I would help of Your love, Your will, and Your way of life. May I do Your will always. I guess I have been doing Your will even when I thought I was all screwed up. I didn't drink or kill myself and I have learned to laugh both at myself and with other people. My kids love me and my wife and I are getting along better. I don't daydream as much and when I do it's not as selfish and I don't have any desire to hurt anyone anymore. Thank You, God. I may not look like a miracle to other people but I sure do to You and me.

"Young man, how can you purport to work a spiritual program with that vulgar mouth?"

"I just do."

*   *   *

Don't Stop Now

*"In sobriety, the only limitations we have
are the ones we put on ourselves."*
Anonymous

About this time in working the Steps, doubts can creep in, unanswerable questions can plague us, and we begin to wonder if we're actually moving forward or if the whole thing is just a joke. Our bodies are back in shape, our lives are intact, and that old mind of ours is clicking away like crazy. Beware. Our heads are not our friends—at least not automatically. We have found ourselves saying things like, "I'm o.k. now. Actually, I would have gone straight with or without the Program. Just so happened it was there." or "Now that I'm recovered, I don't have to be a fanatic about the whole thing. I did the work and it's done." Unfortunately, these kinds of thoughts seldom lead to anything but back to our old path of destruction. We *know* and can *never* forget that our recovery, our new life, is only what we put into it, and that brings us to the maintenance steps.

It shocks us with what ease our heads get into trouble, always in the form of some dishonesty. Rationalization continues to be the one general characteristic we share that produces most of our problems. What *rationalization* means is that we try to give a reason for something that we did or want to do, and think is wrong to do. Because we feel guilty or uncomfortable in some way, we try to make up a good reason for what we did or what we want to do. Most of the time, the reasons we make up sound pretty good. But that doesn't make them true. And even if they were true, bad behavior is still bad behavior.

Step 10:   We continued to take personal inventory, and when we were wrong promptly admitted it.

A consistent or daily inventory keeps us from getting too far off base. A personal awareness of what we say, what we do, and an attempt at correcting any errors immediately will keep us in shape. A girl in our group elaborates:

"I used to always go through phases when I really felt down and never knew why. This drove me up a wall, made me hyper, and then I'd want to escape. Through my daily inventories, I can sort out my feelings, detect growing resentments, and I can keep a space cleared for contact with my HP."

Our thoughts have to be continuously constructive, continuously honest, for life is a continuous process and recovery proves to be part of that continuous process. Each day, an individual meets his own self—in the physical, the mental, or the spiritual phase of his experience. And for our life experience to be one of growing, we must be honest, constructive, and steady.

To keep our head as our friend, we must maintain our growth through discipline and steadiness or we find ourselves in turmoil. We are going to meet problems every day, and then, when we find ourselves in doubt, when we find our emotions bouncing all over the place, or when we find ourselves in panic, we pause and sincerely ask our Higher Power, "What would YOU have me to do today?" Even when we have days that don't bring a crisis on us, we should make that pause at least three times a day and ask the same question. Asking the question should not become a rote exercise. Mean it. And you will gain a protection and guidance you would never have believed possible.

Don't be afraid to explore the areas of prayer and meditation to discover what feels right for you. These are necessary parts of our recovery—yes, the foundation upon which we build and maintain ALL.

Step 11:   We sought through prayer and meditation to improve our conscious contact with God, *as we understood Him,* praying only for knowledge of His will for us and the power to carry that out.

Prayer and meditation hold the contact open so that we can balance our daily experiences, thus balancing our lives. In this way, we keep our recovery in proper perspective. If we get out of balance in any one area, we run the risk of toppling over, even crashing. If we dare to allow the body to do as it pleases, if we allow the mind to be controlled by, "What will my friends say?" and the spirit shelved, only to be displayed at meetings, there *cannot* be anything but confusion. We need guidance, we need direction, of that we have no doubt. And we have to keep asking for it.

Not of ourselves alone can we accomplish this. No human power, no philosophy, no physical vibrations, nor anything else can replace Divine intervention and direction. Nor can we receive such complete love and joy from any other source. A young member of A.A. says:

"It seems to me that the more I stay in touch with my feelings and the more I keep a conscious contact with God, the more balanced my life seems. I can take things that come to me and deal with them on a much more mature level. Often, I am filled with the joy of living, a feeling that I can't explain, but I think it is a gift from God. To be able to comprehend the peace and joy that comes at times is only possible through experience."

And we know that the only way to have the experience is through the disciplined and consistent application of these Twelve Steps.

Taking time out during the day for prayer and meditation doesn't mean that all the joy has to go out of our lives. Taking time to think before we act may cause us to wonder if we should be doing some of the things that we are up to. And our experience cautions us not to engage in any activities with question marks attached. What you don't know might harm you, in other words. But not giving in to everything we want to do does not call for a long-faced, boring type of life. Through God, there is love, joy, laughter, peace, and more attainable in our Fellowships. Even if you've found yourself mis-using our open, extended hand at times and grasping for it at other times, *claim it, claim it now* as your opportunity, and soon you will find the love, peace, and happiness you want.

Another part of our daily program is the protection we seek each morning. Upon arising, before splitting for work or school, we ask, "God, please help me to stay clean and sober today." This works; it really does work for us all. Don't believe for a minute that these simple measures apply only to the mediocre mind and not to you. The truth applies to everyone and the truth of our disease is that we need protection from that first fix, pill, or drink. One only has to think back a minute to remember how well our own measures worked!

There is more to this program than just not getting stoned. We no longer concern ourselves with the world of drugs, but cling to the world of sobriety. The life we have a chance at now is confined only by the boundaries we put on it. Each of us should be aware that a sound personal program, balanced in body, mind, and soul offers far more living potential than any of the trips we have come off in the past.

Kim

*The twenty-four hour rhythm with the sun and moon
was much too simple for her to take part in.*

I cried for freedom like the hungriest child crying for his mother's milk-filled breast, wanting so badly to be me, and not knowing what that me was. So at thirteen, the search was on. And when I found no answers in that number one joint, or number two, or three, and on and on, I searched for more powerful ingredients to capture the feelings those tabs or capsules had stored within them.

I remember my first toke, my first trip, and my first needle rush. I have survived to remember the last of those highs. It's the ones in between that I've conveniently spaced out as conveniently as I had spaced out their destructive powers that dragged me so low. And thanks to some supernatural help, I'm still around to talk about it.

The twenty-four-hour rhythm with the sun and moon was much too simple for me to take part in. After all, I wanted to be free. I wanted to be Kim, and Kim had to be unique. I wouldn't settle for less. So, I transformed mother earth into a mountain, and my destination was to reach the top, and there, to find all the answers. Upward I would climb, each day getting higher and higher.

Alone, I would sit in my candle-lit room, proceeding to stone my mind before going to bed and again before going to school.

For a year I went on this way without much hassle. A few close friends knew. My teachers had their own ideas, which they graciously shared with my parents. And my parents graciously shared their objections with me. That's when I built the brick walls, building them higher and higher, so as not to hear their much too loud voices and over-dramatic lectures. Stone-faced, I hid behind those walls, denying and lying to their questions and accusations. Time went by and lectures became threats, and threats became extreme physical punishment. My parents had reached their limit. My father lost control and left me with bruises a couple of times. I don't mean that to sound so bland. Doubt me not, it was more than our everyday family routine.

For the most part, I had a beautiful family life. My father was a strong, responsible man who spent fifteen years working his way up in his job. My mother appeared perfect—from spotless house to great cook to good seamstress. My brother brought home good grades, won trophies, got his picture in the paper, and my sister was the baby of the family. I didn't fit in with all the excellence. It hurt me and it hurt them. It hurt my father to the point of what looked like madness and I was past the point of caring. I screamed my hatred, wishing them to be dead, always crying to be free.

Then came Jerry. Along with him came new friends. New friends in old clothes with free spirits. My old friends were calling me back, back to their social trips with hypocritical overtones, so I thought. I'm not saying my fate changed because my friends changed. No, I think that's the biggest joke of all. My old friends were smoking pot and eating acid, too. But only we knew. With Jerry and my new friends, secrecy didn't matter anymore.

That year my parents told me that we were moving to South Dakota. My feelings were mixed. In Denver I had Jerry and all my friends. I was born and raised in this town. I knew no other. But I felt that I was in a rut and wanted a change, and I thought this might be the answer. In the end, we all agreed to go, and my parents bought a bar and house, and we moved to the Black Hills. Jerry was evidently in love because he moved there, too, renting our cabin. Everything was going A-o.k. My parents were working so hard to make the bar work that they didn't have time to make the family work, and suddenly, there was a change all right—from one extreme to the other.

I truly don't know what happened. Things were going all right, but suddenly they turned around, and Dad and I ended up in the boxing ring again. I managed to jump through the ropes and get out the door, this time not to return.

Jerry and I hitch-hiked back to Colorado on an everday acid trip. My only thought seemed to be to get as messed-up as I possibly could. After a few months, I called my parents, told them Jerry and I were married, and that I wanted to be left alone. We had not married, and I'm sure my parents knew, but I was well taken care of and out of their hair.

Jerry's job paid well, and after school, I worked also. We rented a beautiful house, bought a new car, and he spoiled me with lots and lots of drugs.

The first year went smoothly, but, of course, it went smoothly because things went my way. As far as Jerry was concerned, they went my way too long. He started getting down on me for missing too much school, doing too many drugs, and he wanted me to quit my job. He began to question my love—was it for him or for his drugs? I had no answer. Somehow, like my father, he ended up visualizing me as a punching bag, too.

After a year of that, I walked out another door never to return, and my excursion up the mountain continued.

The way I was living, the next thing that happened was inevitable: I became pregnant. My parents reminded me I was not yet seventeen and they insisted that I had to live with them. At first I decided to have the baby, but then concluded that it would be wrong to have this child. I called Jerry, although he was not the father, and made arrangements to abort.

I was far along, and the shot I was given induced me into labor for a twenty-four-hour period. They couldn't relieve the pain too much or it would also stop the labor, and, through the pain, I prayed to keep a grasp on what sanity I had left. Both the emotional and physical pain seemed undeserved for even Satan himself, and finally, the nurse left. It was over. And my drug use, so I thought.

After the abortion, I built my brick walls high enough never to love again, never to hurt again, but not high enough to keep guilt away. My next two years of acid trips all related to that incident.

My next hit of purple micro-dot left me high, it seemed, forever. In my bedroom, I looked at the floor only to see it stained with blood. I realized it was the acid messing with my head, and I decided to go to sleep and space this trip off. But I couldn't sleep and I lost almost total contact with reality. My family was sleeping, but I sensed that they were dead. Worst of all, I thought I had killed them. I wasn't sure what was going on. I locked our house pets into my bedroom so I wouldn't harm them, and roamed the house. After a few mintues of this, I grasped a little reality and knew I needed help. I went to my brother's room, woke him, and told him I was tripping and not to let me hurt anyone.

I tripped for over forty-eight hours, and my brother stayed with me the whole time. After finally coming down, I stayed home for eight days, away from my friends and away from drugs. Big deal! Believe it or not, I was soon back at it again. I had to find that freedom which I knew was waiting out there somewhere for me.

Like some sick, wounded animal, I continued up my mountain. I ran everything that would flow into my vein. From coke to wine to tequila. I never ran across a tab I couldn't crush, dilute, and bring through a used cigarette filter if I had to.

Doing things like this, reality wasn't mine to have. It was there only to make me cry. I reached for it, if only for it to take me to my grave. From being so drugged, I had actually planned for my death, accepting it willingly, and yet wished it would not take me away when I was like this. Eventually I would come down, swearing never to trip again, and within hours I would be high, still wanting to be free.

That is behind me now. I have found my answer in sobriety and it wasn't on top of the mountain. In fact, that mountain doesn't even exist anymore. I'm part of reality now, and reality to me is acceptance of life without drugs. There *can be no* freedom for me with drugs, *for they control.* I'm content now doing what I want to do, not what the drugs make me want to do. They no longer control my life. I call that freedom.

My short time of sobriety has answered more questions than six years of drugs could. I have learned not to look for the answers but rather to try to understand the questions. I did not do this alone, because we are unable to find sobriety alone. What I did do was to find the courage to accept the fact that I needed help and then to ask for this help. I've admitted that I'm powerless; I have sought a Higher Power and this Higher Power has made things a lot easier in my life. For now, I accept what is to be.

As I've said, I was unable to do it alone, something I would have never admitted a year ago. It almost seems I didn't want help, but a friend came to me—a real friend—and told me about a program he had gone to. I was pleased he had found something to help him, but I felt it wasn't the answer I was looking for. I didn't have a clear idea what it was I so desperately wanted to find, but I was sure this wasn't it. I eventually went to the meeting more for him than myself, which in turn I found was "wrong." I then learned of the things I would have to give up and quickly decided that I would not do this for anyone but myself. I can't think of anyone more important than myself to sacrifice so much for.

To me A.A. and N.A. are not just programs, they are new ways of life. That's the only way I can explain it, and the only thing I needed was to be honest. It sounds so simple. For me it wasn't. I had bricked in all my honesty by building those walls as a child—guarding against my feelings of fear and hurt. These walls were torn down and I cried while they tumbled. It hurt! I was so afraid of what I might see behind them, and all that I found was me, that Kim I'd been searching for all along, and I *can* accept her for what she is and in spite of what she has done. It's so much easier not playing those crazy games anymore. I wanted so badly to be unique. Now I feel that I truly am. I feel just as special as any person and the things I've given up to be with my A.A. friends have been worth it all. My cries were answered and I was set free, honestly free.

Sobriety to me is a high that doesn't interfere with my love for God, or whatever you want to call the Higher Power. I call it "God" because I know of no other name. I only know of its existence. I mostly believe because I don't want to be alone, and standing in the middle of thousands of people won't give me the security I get from this supernatural force. I simply like the idea of a God being there.

The crazy thing about my previous denial of God's existence is that I accepted the existence of evil forces. What I'm about to express may start shrinks looking for me, but I swear my experiences were real, as real as any force can be. I had this freaked out paranoia of demons. They were constantly bugging me, and they didn't care if I was alone or not.

One night (during the time I lived with Jerry) I awoke and couldn't move. I was aware of my surroundings but felt like something inside my mind was preventing me from moving. I wanted to scream "help" or anything, but nothing would come out of my mouth. This lasted for a few seconds, and, then, with a jerk, all my faculties were returned. I was, of course, terrified. I woke Jerry and told him. He looked at me as if I were a mad woman. I refused to ask for help from a God because I was afraid it might challenge these forces—and my faith wasn't strong enough to take on this kind of challenge.

After a few months of this, Jerry finally realized there was definitely something weird going on. We were sitting on the rug just talking about off the wall things. And he gave me that mad woman look again as he said "Man, there is really something weird going on in you." I didn't know what he was referring to, but it scared the hell out of me. The next day when I got home from school he'd bought me a gift. I opened it and it was a Black Hills Gold Cross. I don't know what you would actually call crazy forces such as I think I experienced. All I know is that I like God's way a lot better.

One thing that helped my attitude about A.A. and N.A. meetings is the availability of different groups, one to suit any mood. If I just put as much effort into finding meetings as I did into going to bars, I will be way ahead of the game. These days I don't care how far I have to drive to get to these meetings, and I have met some fantastic people in A.A. and N.A. I don't have to be anything special for them to accept me. I am what I am. They are who they are and I like that.

It is true that because my sobriety comes first now, I have to give up some people I have known as friends. At one time, these people meant more to me than I meant to myself. But that got me nowhere. They love drugs more than they love me—or themselves. I don't blame them; I still love and care for them. I always will. But I have to live with myself, not with them. I need my ability to think and I cherish my sanity. I give them the freedom to be who they are, as they must allow me to be who I am. Who knows? Maybe one day they will find the freedom I have found.

Mike

*He swore he'd never touch that abominable
liquid that he felt had cheated him out of
so much of his childhood.*

A few people have told me that my alcoholism was inevitable from the beginning. As I recall, I had a rough childhood. My father left when I was about a year old, and my mother was ill-equipped to raise three kids alone. Her hampered attempts took their toll on my psyche. To this day I still shudder when I think of how many times we three little kids were in a strange man's house. Our mother would be screaming in the next room. Bottles would be crashing against the wall. We'd hear shuffling and men's voices. My anguish at these moments was indescribable. All I wanted was not to hear, not to know. I just wanted to make it all stop. Something inside of my body would tell me that one way out was to reach for a bottle of Ripple wine and chug-a-lug the juice inside. But I didn't, and eventually I would fall asleep and be at peace.

In time my mother got so bad in her own drinking that relatives took me in. As I got older I forgot about a lot of my early traumas, but I swore I'd never touch that abominable liquid that I felt had cheated me out of so much in my childhood. By the time I got to high school I was quite withdrawn, so the counselor said. I wouldn't participate in any activities willingly, and ditched them every chance I got. Whereas I desperately needed understanding and emotional help, school only managed to bring me more pain and anguish. Even though I swore I'd never touch the drink that I had grown to despise because of its power to transform my mother into a female Mr. Hyde, as I had witnessed so many times, I found myself experimenting with alcohol at seventeen because I just had to find out what was its amazing attraction to adults.

One weekend, a friend told me his dad had gone out of town and asked if I wanted to try some one-hundred-eighty-one proof rum he found in the liquor cabinet. My chance had arrived. This was the perfect opportunity to satisfy my curiosity about the attraction liquor held for adults.

At first we tried to drink it straight. Needless to say, that didn't work at all, so we started to cut it with water until we settled on a 50-50 solution. It was hard to stomach but I kept drinking glass after glass because I wanted the "experiment" to be successful. When the rum bottle started to look frighteningly low, we filled it back up with water, put it away in the liquor cabinet, and drove back to my house. The last thing I remember was falling backward in my living room. I woke up periodically that night feeling like fire was burning my throat with every breath I took, and I didn't feel well for five days.

Instead of taking heed from the results of my experiment by writing off alcohol as too toxic for my body, I decided I must not have experimented properly. I was determined to do it as many times as I needed until I discovered the true, alluring properties of alcohol. After a few more tries, I finally did discover the amazing curative powers of inebriation. Thereafter events in my life became hazy.

If alcohol could make me feel strong, powerful, appealing and confident at parties while I was indulging, then, to what heights could I climb with other drugs? Being in the midst of a drug revolution made it easy for us kids to jump right into drug use. We tried smoking banana peels, eating oregano and jimson weed seeds, and popping amyl nitrate. Anything to get a high.

A girl once invited me to a party, and I asked her what kind of a party it would be. What I really meant was, "Will there be any booze there?" When I ascertained that there wouldn't be, I declined. I then asked her if she drank. To her "No," I replied that she didn't know what she was missing. When I left, I remember thinking how strange she was. How could anyone be so out of it so as not to have discovered the joys of drinking? She must have been a real deadbeat at a party. Virtually everyone in the world drank.

Without realizing it, I had filtered out of my life all of the people that didn't drink or use. And then the thought came to me that it was just as likely that the non-users had filtered me out of *their* lives by avoiding me. Oddly enough I still nurtured a small spark inside my gut that wanted very badly to be successful. I rebelled against authority in small ways, but never enough to get in big trouble. I stayed away from demonstrations, burglaries, and hard drugs. When my sister ran away to Haight-Ashbury and implored me to join her in her new found bliss, I declined, much too conservative for that radical a move.

Instead I enrolled in junior college after high school graduation. I had taken a psychology class in high school, and it excited and intrigued me. Psychology was the only subject that I had ever taken that I thought was relevant. It not only asked the right questions, it also promised many of the answers to the problems and dilemmas I faced in my life. I chose it as my major.

At that time the draft board was inducting all eligible males, but I knew that if I maintained fifteen units of passing college credit every semester, I would temporarily escape the draft through a II-S student deferment. As the names of war dead were appearing in our hometown newspaper, I recognized some of them. I also heard stories from returning veterans. The idea of being sent to Vietnam to be killed, carved up, and hung in a tree by the Viet Cong was very distasteful to me to say the least. Yet as determined as I was to stay in school and do well, my grades steadily declined. I could always study later, after I smoked a joint or had a few beers with a friend. I got to the point where I was dropping more classes than I was keeping.

Getting involved with the police became an integral part of life with my girl-friend. We fought constantly. Friends told me she was too wild and to find someone else, but I only resented their meddling in my affairs. Eventually she and I got busted big. We were smoking pot in a car on a dirt road in the foothills one night with two friends. The police had watched our headlights move up the road and shut off. They waited thirty minutes before coming up to investigate. By then we were good and high.

When we saw them approach, our friends collected the dope and started running away. I grabbed my girlfriend and we ran to my car. Along the dirt road, up into the foothills, we drove. The red lights were getting closer in my rear view mirror. I knew we couldn't escape in the car, and all I could think of was that someone had once told me that anyone who got busted and was found to have marijuana in his blood through police drug tests would never be accepted by a graduate school. The spark in me that wanted to be successful was crying out, "Oh God, please don't let this be happening to me!" I had to get away or I'd never be able to go to graduate school.

I stopped the car, grabbed my girl, and started running. She kept falling, and I kept yanking her back up to keep us running. Eventually she fell and screamed, "I think I broke my leg!" I picked her up and started running again. She struggled to get loose and told me to put her down. It was no use. She didn't want to go on and begged me to stay with her. "If you love me, you won't leave me," she cried. I had to decide between her and graduate school. Graduate school won out. All I could say was, "Don't let them catch you; stay hidden in the bushes."

I ran through the hills barefoot and the bushes were tearing at my clothes. When I felt I had run far enough, I stopped and hid under a bush. As I was catching my breath, I started to survey the scene. I could see vehicles moving up the fireroads. A large searchlight was combing the hills and portable lights were jogging into the hills at various points as if they were being carried by search parties. I still vividly recall the feeling that night up on the hill when I was all alone in the dark: cold, tired, and hurting. The combination of chemicals in my brain combined with the bizarre scenario unfolding before me to make the whole affair seem like a bad dream. Fearing God had abandoned me, I looked upward into the night sky and pleaded with Him to let me wake up and make the nightmare go away.

After a few hours the lights turned around and started to retreat, leaving only the cold night and me—with a few weeds to use as a warm covering. As the anesthetizing properties of the marijuana started to wear off, my body began to hurt all over. Morning came very slowly, but finally it was light. I tried to stand up on feet that were swollen and sore. I put one foot forward to take a step. As I put pressure on it, I recoiled with pain. Eventually I was able to start walking by taking each step a little at a time. Now that I was thinking straight, I realized the only rational course of action was to go home. My father was a policeman. Because I agreed to cooperate with the authorities, he was able to get me off the hook. The whole story was kept out of the papers, and I was so grateful that I quit using drugs for about six months—although I continued to drink.

My life continued to deteriorate as I lost my job and stopped attending classes. My day centered around the case of beer I managed to obtain every day, and I noticed that my hands would shake when I tried to pick up a cup of coffee or light a cigarette. I sometimes wondered if I was o.k. Crazily, I concluded I must be. After all, I was only nineteen; alcoholism happened only when one got older.

The network of problems I had created in my personal relationships seemed insurmountable, and I began to feel that it was time to split from my family. My dad had retired on a spread up north. I had visited him on past occasions and it was a drinking paradise. That was where I belonged. I told all my friends I was going to British Honduras to throw them off the track and headed north.

That move marked the beginning of the end of my alcoholism and drug dependency. I didn't realize what was happening, but most of my behavior in life had become reduced to seeking out the next high. We'd pull the seats out of cars looking for change, and we'd cash our pop bottles to buy another gallon of Red Mountain wine. We'd befriend anyone who just got paid and had enough money to keep us supplied for a while or else looked like a promising prospect for future sustenance.

One usual Saturday night I sat in one of the bars when a cowboy began to poke fun at a friend of mine who stuttered, and I gallantly rose to defend him. The cowboy beat me up pretty badly but no one lifted a finger to help me. When I woke up the next morning all swollen and hung over, I asked myself if possibly something might be going wrong in my life. Knowing that I was moving hopelessly away from my life image of success, I told myself I must be just having a few bad breaks, that things would start coming together. So I continued to drink and use and continued to find myself waking up in strange places without knowing how I got there. On weekends I would hitch-hike to San Francisco, take opium, hashish, pot, LSD, booze, and pills either separately or mixed, however they came. My thinking deteriorated as I became a member of another realm. Even communication changed. I couldn't talk to "straights" or non-users, but as a matter of fact, I had such a good rapport with fellow druggies that we rarely had to talk to each other at all. We could sense what each other meant with only a nod, gesture, or monosyllabic word.

My girlfriend at the time could drink with the best of them, and, in my craziness, I was a bit worried about her. We went down to L.A. to visit my mother who had joined Alcoholics Anonymous. It was the best news that I had heard from her, because God only knew how long she had needed it. Flatteringly, she called me aside to be privy to a plan to expose my girlfriend to A.A. My mother said she'd heard my girl was quite a drinker, and I confirmed the reports. The idea was to get her to an A.A. meeting so she would know where to get help in case she recognized problems with drinking in the future. My mother asked me to tell my girlfriend that she wanted us to drive her to a meeting where we would then decide it would be easier to stay and sit through it rather than go all the way back home, just to return again. I thought it was a great idea and fell right into my mother's plan for my exposure to A.A.

I heard some incredible things at that meeting. People were describing their lives, thinking, and drinking patterns in a way that fit me to a T, but the full force of that realization was too much for me to absorb that night although the things they said at that meeting kept ringing in my ears for weeks afterward. Everytime I picked up a drink, I couldn't help examining my behavior and comparing it to the patterns they had described at the A.A. meeting.

Then my friends in San Francisco had started using heroin and I knew it was only a matter of time before I would be using it also. One day, during what can only be described as the beginning of a month-long spiritual intervention into the destructive course on which I had set my life, the fog parted in my head. It was long enough for me to objectively see my situation and options. I had an image of myself walking down a path that forked in front of me. One road led to heroin and ultimate death. The other led to total abstinence and a long struggle for survival.

At that moment I had to make what was to be the most momentous decision in my life. Strangely, I was in a place where I didn't particularly care which road I took, as they both had their pros and cons. It was virtually a tossup. Heroin would be easy at the start. All I had to do was say yes and it would be available. Later I would have some rough times looking for my next fix, but that stage wouldn't last long. Eventually it would lead to oblivion and death. The other road would be very painful in the beginning and require a lifetime of effort but would return more and more dividends as time went on. Which road would I take? I looked at the heroin road and tuned into the feeling in my gut about it. I heard a tiny sound. What was it? I concentrated more. The sound grew and I began to recognize it as the voice of that once burning desire to be successful and to be a contributor to the world. I realized that I'd almost extinguished that desire with drugs.

After much deliberation, I chose the life path. I wanted to live. I wanted to make it! I would go for broke to be a success. I dug up an old letter from my sister, who had previously joined A.A. and N.A. from my dresser drawer that I had stuffed in there months before. It said, "When you are ready, come to Denver. We are waiting for you." I hadn't known what she meant at the time, but now I did. I was ready. I gathered up all of my belongings—clothes, books, equipment, furniture, and all. I piled everything high in the yard and doused the pile with kerosene. I set it on fire and ritualistically danced around the blaze. I was saying good-bye to my past. I didn't want anything to be left behind to come back for. I borrowed $40.00 and set out for Denver.

I'll always remember that month in Denver as one of near bliss. I stayed in a basement with my sister, worked the grave yard shift as a dishwasher at a coffee house on the corner, and attended three A.A. meetings a day. It was the spring of 1970, I was twenty, and finally didn't have a care in the world. The weight of a one-ton block had been lifted from my shoulders. There was hope. Success had not deliberately evaded me; I had been sick. I wasn't at fault. There was nothing intrinsically wrong with me. The only thing that I had to do to be all right was just not drink! Joy and hope overwhelmed me, and I was just happy to be in a place where I felt I belonged. I was so happy I didn't even care at this point what was being said at the meetings and only absorbed what slipped into my head through the ideas I could catch. I wrote letters and sent literature (with the important points underlined) to all the alcoholics I knew back home. I was on a crusade to share with the world the benefits of my new-found utopia. So what if they never answered my letters. I was sure they'd soon come around to recognizing the value of the program.

But my romance with the program was cut short. The draft board had caught up with me, and I had three options: 1) Allow myself to be inducted into the army to fight and quite possibly be killed. 2) Burn my draft card as some of my friends had done and go to prison. 3) Leave the country.

On the one hand, I fancied myself too civilized to regress back to the barbaric level of war. And besides, if everyone like myself refused to fight, wars would not exist. On the other hand, the thought of incarceration was unbearable and I found it particularly unnerving to permanently abandon the culture and land that I knew, loved, and belonged to. They were not what I'd call a very satisfying set of options.

Making a calcualted risk, I decided my best choice was to enlist in the Navy, and the only thing that got me through the military was A.A. meetings. My credo for maintaining sobriety evolved into, *"NEVER* ACCEPT THAT DRINK RIGHT NOW; *ALWAYS* GO TO ANOTHER MEETING."* That principle became imprinted on my mind. No matter how bad things went or what happened, I would never take a drink at that time and would always go to another meeting.

The quality of my sobriety was questionable at best. After release from the Navy, I felt the need of more than the program to deal with my deep inner turmoil. I bounced around in therapies from Encounter Groups to Primal Scream. They all helped somewhat, but I never would let myself forget where my sobriety came from and I always stayed close to a meeting.

Growth seemed to be coming slowly. Even as I prayed for patience and guidance, I found it particularly hard to turn my life over to God. But with each little bit that I did manage to turn over, He paid me back with dividends.

Everything in my life has been steadily improving from personal relationships to personal accomplishments. Today I can say I am married to a wonderful woman from a fine family. I also graduated from a university *summa cum laude* and am finishing a master's degree in experimental psychology. I am looking forward to applying to a Ph.D. program and starting a happy, healthy family. I guess God did hear my prayer up on that hill that night, after all. He just had to wait for me to let Him answer it.

5

Free Money

*"All I've got has been given to me.
All I have to do to lose it, is to keep it."
Anonymous*

Now that we have your attention, we can confess that this chapter has nothing to do with any free money, although one of our people did remark, "Just look at all that money you can spend on yourself, now that you're not blowing it on your crutches to hide from reality." We had several very sound titles, all of which were appropriate, none of which we could get a majority vote on; they were:

Reaching Out

Open Hands

Give it Away to Keep it

Saving Our Own Ass

Twelfth Stepping

Someone Needs Your Help

These titles refer to the final and most enlightening step of all, Step Twelve. Reaching this step breaks through the discouragements, wavering attitudes, and the limitations of the addictions syndrome. Through this final step we continuously hold fast to the purpose set in our hearts by the previous eleven steps. We are satisfied with nothing less than living life in full measure and come to realize that living life in full measure is probably our greatest challenge. Our foundation has been built, and we fulfill the challenge with great joy and anticipation. The Twelfth Step insures our continuous growth and its simplicity represents *freedom* to us.

Step 12:   Having had a spiritual awakening as a result of these steps, we tried to carry this message to addicts and to practice these principles in all our affairs.

Spiritual awakening? Now just how does one describe a spiritual awakening? Does this imply a great expection or a small one? We would ask that you don't "expect" anything at all. The spiritual experience can be viewed as a change in consciousness, *in whatever form* it unfolds for you. One of our people explained his experience as "... realizing that I didn't need to kill myself to have something better, a better state of mind. Now, having a better state of mind, I can have a better state of affairs." *That's* a spiritual experience? Yep, it sure is. Another member described it this way:

"I was praying desperately for a sponsor—no one seemed to fit the bill. One day, I walked into an A.A. club and there sat a woman with seventeen years sobriety—a woman I despised. She seemed pompous and shallow to me. Suddenly I was unable to walk past and a voice ran through my head, *'Ask her to be your sponsor.'* 'Hold on a minute,' I protested, 'I don't even *like* her.' I tried to move past but still couldn't. 'Can't we negotiate?' I wailed inwardly. No dice— I couldn't move. 'O.k.' I surrendered. I asked her to be my sponsor and she said, 'No!' 'Some joke,' I muttered as I walked away. That night the lady called me and having re-thought the matter, she agreed to be my sponsor. All I can say today is that there couldn't have been a more perfect sponsor for me and it seems that I had nothing to do with it!"

Now *that* sounds more like a spiritual awakening. Well, maybe so. But there are no necessary ingredients; you will get what you need, whether it is a booming voice from the skies, a quiet voice from within, or simply a brand new thought.

The second part of this step is what we term Twelfth Step work or "twelfth stepping:" "We tried to carry this message to alcoholics."

We often tend to be evangelistic at first and we impetuously set out to save the world from the ravages of mind-affecting chemicals. We can become so overwrought in our efforts that some members wind up twelfth stepping people who don't even have our disease! When the enthusiasm mellows, there are some guidelines and suggestions you may consider following.

Members of A.A. and N.A. with long-term sobriety teach us to share our experience, our strength, and our hope. We tell *our* stories of what it was like, what happened, and what it's like now. After all, we have no stories or wisdom to convey other than what happened in our own experience. The Fellowships also teach us that we are on twenty-four-hour call to anyone who sincerely seeks our help. Remember those we needed were there when we reached out. Our nine guidelines for helping another with our illness:

1) Stick to your own story. This way you cannot say anything "wrong."
2) Always try to twelfth step in pairs, especially late at night.
3) It is best for guys to twelfth step guys and women to twelve step women.
4) NO "Thirteenth Stepping!" (That's going a step further than just helping with their drug problem and deciding to help with the sex problem you just diagnosed.)
5) Avoid playing one-upsmanship with new or potential members. (Who used the most drugs isn't important.)
6) Don't patronize, preach, condemn, or condone.
7) You are not a professional; an "I don't know" for an answer to a question can keep you on an honest, open track.
8) Quietly ask for guidance before beginning.
9) Don't forget the humor, the smile, and the open arms welcome.

When working with others we remember that we are not doing it for them; we are doing it to save ourselves. Nothing brings us back to basics faster than seeing a shattered and shaking sick one going down fast while fighting the disease. One of our members said:

"I used to worry about whether I'd be any help. What should I say? I found if I just turned it over to my HP and let Him use me as a channel— things worked out and I felt good about it. I'm not going out to save them, but to save me."

Twelfth stepping "happens" in varied ways. Once people begin to notice the changes in you, they will start asking you to talk to the kids they might be concerned with. Also, it is helpful to call your local Central Office* and offer to aid any young people who phone in. You might also decide to twelfth step through letters. There are a number of recovering young people isolated, not from A.A. or N.A., but from peers, and as you know, we are valuable to each other. A.A. Central Office in New York is the place to contact for letter twelfth step work.

When any institution elicits our support, we do not turn our backs, even if there are prior resentments towards them or even if we feel embarrassed and

---

*A Central Office is a local clearing house and information center for A.A. and N.A. in most major cities. It can be located by referring to the telephone book. Look under "Alcoholics Anonymous" or "Narcotics Anonymous."

inadequate. We are in a unique positon to help potential members in schools, churches, correction centers, and the like, because we speak their language, rap, slang. These kids will often listen to you more quickly and more intently than they will to someone from the establishment.

Finally, we are told to carry the message. *Nothing* is said about delivering it. In other words, we carry the message by being a living example of sobriety and sharing our program whenever possible. But cramming it down people's throats and giving lectures on the evils of dope is definitely, a No-No and will accomplish little except to frustrate you and turn off kids who may desperately need our help.

The third part of the final step is "to practice these principles in our our affairs." Principles? What principles? These Steps are a principled way of life encompassing honestly, open-mindedness, willingness to learn, responsibility, and love—we know that you can identify many more principles. The key to the idea is *practice*. We practice these principles in all our affairs. That means with parents as well as friends, at school as well as at meetings, with a date as well as a sponsor, and yes, that even refers to the police (or "pigs" if you're not past this phase yet).

If, *after* completing these simple steps, you do not have our advantage of being able to attend a young people's group, there is nothing to prevent you from starting one. Talk to the closest central office and tell them of your intentions, share your hopes. Visit numerous meetings in your area and encourage alateens and older A.A.'s and/or N.A.'s to attend. You must be prepared to be responsible and to commit yourself for a least six months. That will mean opening the meeting each week whether or not people show up, having coffee or tea ready, and making program literature available.

Above all, be patient. It sometimes takes a while for groups to catch on. And remember, even if a group doesn't actually hang together, your hard work will pay off because you will be sitting there sober!

Our program of recovery, our present existence, our continued support stems from the older A.A. and N.A. groups. We in no way neglect or isolate ourselves from them.

Realistically looking ahead a few years, we are going to be them. The Fellowships are in no way exclusive; they are open to anyone who has a desire to stop using; age, sex, color, or creed are not barriers in relating. Our disease is the same, our feelings are the same, and most importantly, our solution is the same. It is apparent that our common bond is not in the disease, but in the solution. We all have found the same way out.

Joy

*Whereas she used to be paranoid in
a negative sense, she is now
paranoid in a positive sense.*

My name is Joy, and I am a fifteen-year-old recovering drug addict. I never thought of myself as an addict; I just took drugs. Funny that I should end up an addict, because when I was a little girl, I was so against any kind of drugs that I used to punch pinholes in my mother's cigarettes and pour her booze down the sink. A terrible thing to do to someone hooked on tobacco and alcohol!

I remember how getting high made me feel the first time. I was o.k., not different, and in touch with other people. Before the drugs, I had always felt as if I were from another planet, alien and cut off from people. Feeling that nobody on earth understood me, my problems, or my emotions left me with an awful sense of loneliness, but when I got high, I felt cushioned from the world, life was easier to cope with, and I could pretend I didn't care what other people thought of me. Drifting off to a world of my own that did not include the world's pettiness and discomfort, I felt I had a grand mission in life—I was supposed to help humanity. Maybe I was Jesus reincarnated as a girl. Or I thought that probably I was really on a much higher plane than other people were, and *that's* why I couldn't understand them and they couldn't understand me. The reason why I couldn't fulfill my grand mission in life was that people held me back. They simply didn't know who I was; they were in a vast plot against me. It was the crucifixion of Jesus all over again!

After using pot daily for some time, I felt the call to bigger and better things, and thus, discovered acid. Where pot had given me a taste of a fresher, cleaner world, acid made me a god in control of that world. With acid, I had found my high, I had a feeling of perfection in the universe. The trees, the people, and my mind were all in harmony. I loved everyone and everything, and they loved me back. There was power flowing through me and everything was under control. I was in command, I could manage my life. I decided, after a time, that if acid was so good, maybe there was something better, so I went to find it. Although I never did find anything better, I surely did look.

In the meantime, because of my search, my grades had hit bottom, and school had become a bad trip, so I quit. My mother and I were fighting all the time, and she ended up kicking me out of the house. A friend of mine talked her family into taking me in, but after three weeks there, I got kicked out again —this time for being on acid, and for other crap I pulled while I was on drugs. So there I was—no home, no family—just me and my acid sitting in the snow. I felt very lost and alone, and quite sorry for myself. I remember thinking, ''God, if you'll just get me out of this, I'll never touch another hit of acid the rest of my life.'' Even at that time, however, I still couldn't see that the drugs were causing my problems. I just felt that I had been kicked out because I had been dumb enough to have gotten caught.

As I sat there in the snow, who should appear from nowhere but the lady who got me high the first time. She took me in to live with her and her two small kids. What looked like a good break actually was the beginning of the end for me. It was straight down—and fast—from there on. I had all the drugs I wanted at her house. I began to deal with her, got loaded with her everyday, and got into shoplifting with her on a steady basis. There was nobody to hassle me and I felt I was finally free for the first time in my life. It was later I found that the price of my ''freedom'' was total responsibility for her house and her kids. For six months, I just sat in the house, looked after her kids and got high. I was going through a lid a day, and about three hits of acid a week, besides cocaine whenever I could get it. Boy, I was really free, huh?

After being caught many times for shoplifting and ''always'' being able to con my way out of any serious consequences, I landed in Juvenile Hall. Being in jail was a drag, but in my way, I was proud that I had finally made it. I had made the grade. I was a big girl now.

About a week after I got out of Juvenile Hall, I landed right back in again for shoplifting again. This time, I had three charges of shoplifting against me, I thought my mother had given up on me, and the lady I was living with couldn't help me without sticking her own neck out. The Chief of Police had promised me he would *personally* see that I was sent to the reformatory. I got a hollow, scared feeling in my gut that spelled ''desperate.'' It was then that I remembered what my mother who had been in A.A. for over four years used to say about ''Let Go and Let God.'' What did I have to lose? All I had was me, and I didn't want me anymore. My first prayer was not fancy, just honest: "God, if you want my life, take it, 'cause I don't like me anymore." The way from there has been straight up. It all happened so fast I couldn't believe it. The next day, I was transferred to a youth receiving center, and after a weekend and a day there, I went home to live with my mother and her A.A. husband.

I began going to about four A.A. meetings a week, reading the literature, and trying to use the Twelve Steps in my life. An N.A. meeting started and I went there. However, there were not enough N.A. meetings and I saw that I still needed the help of A.A.

How can I go to A.A. when I have not really drunk very much alcohol in my life? Well, I look at it like this: One beer would make me physically ill, dizzy, disoriented, unable to walk and very uncomfortable. I did not like the high I got from booze. It made me feel more alone than I did when I was sober. I was looking for something to make me feel good, and booze did not make me feel good. Drugs made me feel good. The search was the same as the alcoholic's, but the road was different. The feelings I had were the exact feelings the kids in A.A. talked about. It's just that booze was what got them where they wanted to go, and drugs were what got me to where I wanted to go. We have to remember that the *solution* is the most important thing. Booze is a drug, the same as acid or pot. I am powerless over all intoxicants, and my life became unmanageable. That is all I need to remember to get the relief promised by this Program.

I believe that alcoholism is a disease that can lie dormant in a person for years, before he actually starts to drink. I think the disease has more to do with the way a person thinks and acts than it does with the way he drinks. Alcoholism is the disease for which drinking is a temporary out. Booze and other drugs allow a person to escape from the disease within him for a little while, but that person always has to come back to his disease when he comes down. A.A. does not offer an escape from problems, but it allows a person to stay straight and work on his problems—in his right mind. A.A. teaches us how to be sober, happy, and free. I must keep in my mind that one hit of a joint will start me right back into the old times just as one drink for an alcoholic is a giant step right back to the bottle.

So what is it like now that I'm not doing drugs, and am trying to put the Program into my life? When I was living with the lady and her kids, I really resented my mother and hated her because she was happy and I wasn't. I did my best to make her as unhappy as I was. When I hit my bottom, though, my mind was opened enough to decide that if I couldn't make her unhappy like me, I would allow her to teach me how to be happy. I started to listen to her instead of spacing her out, and discovered that she and her husband are really together people.

Now, I want to talk a little about God. All my life I was searching for a God who would say I was right in what I was doing. I have sought that God in Christianity, Buddhism, and Judaism, trying to bring God down to my level so that I could feel o.k. with what I was doing. Now I see that the way I was living was not good for me, and therefore God would never say it was o.k. God wants good for me; my job is to allow Him to give it to me. In our group, we believe that everyone has to arrive at his very own concept of God. I call my God a "partner." I can understand the idea of a partner a lot better than I can understand the idea of God as a father. My real father is a rather cold man who only loves money and prestige. He left me when I was a baby and never kept in touch or let me get close to him. A partner, on the contrary, is someone who likes you and won't hurt you. My partner will stick with me, believe in me and back me up. My partner only expects honesty of me, wanting me to tell him the truth, no matter how rough that truth might be. He runs the show because He knows more than I do and is more powerful than I am. Things turn out well when He does it, and they always turn out rotten when I alone do it.

You see, I am still "paranoid"—except that now I have what I like to call "positive paranoia." I really believe that there is a vast plot *for* me to succeed!

When I came into this Program, it seemed to me that life would be a real bitch if I couldn't get loaded. I find now, though, that I'm happier than I've ever been. Before, fun used to be just sitting around and getting loaded. Now I have a lot of fun going to dances, on picnics, and just sitting around after a meeting, drinking coffee, rapping and telling jokes. I find the program is not the bitch I thought it would be, because my partner never lays anything on me that He and I can't handle together. It's a good feeling to know that my partner goes with me everywhere—even to school. If things get rough at school, I just go any place where I can be by myself and have a little talk with Him. He comes through everytime. I used to think that only the kids who got high were cool, but now I find that those kids bore me. The kids who don't get high have more to say, do more things, and are a lot more fun to be around. I have made many friends with them. Nobody likes a drooping dopehead, except other drooping dopeheads.

I now have something to give other people and I'm feeling better about myself all the time. I never have to be alone again, and I'm beginning to really feel like a "Joy" again! For that I am very grateful.

Personal Relationships

When people made me unhappy, my first inclination
was to beat the hell out of them.
The Program has taught me to THINK!
Phil

One of the biggest, all-time phoney excuses that we have used for getting loaded is the hassles and pressures of day-to-day living. More often than not these hassles and pressures are associated with personal relationships. Let's face it, a hang nail is not exactly a hassle and a thunderstorm is not exactly a pressure. *But* being on the verge of expulsion from school *is* a hassle and parents jumping on your back constantly is a pressure and these examples involve people, *i.e.,* personal relationships.

Before we go any further, we need to get one thing straight. We do not get stoned because of hassles and pressures in our lives. We get stoned because we suffer from the addictions syndrome. Any other reason we tell ourselves is only an excuse for doing what we intended to do anyway. We know that "problems" do not cause our disease for two very sound reasons.

1. *Everybody* has problems, but not everybody is an alcoholic or an addict.
2. *We remember* all the times we got high to have fun, to enjoy sex, when we were bored, to be a part of the crowd, because it was our birthday, because it was Sunday, because it was Monday, because it was any day at all.

We have come to realize that personal relationships do not get us stoned, but many times they sure seem to cause us a lot of pain. Negative emotions act like a poison in our system and throw us completely off balance; they cause us to lose touch with our ideals and threaten our conscious contact with HP. This loss of contact we cannot afford, so a certain amount of emotional examination is in order. Mainly, the emotions that are examined are dealt with in Steps Four through Nine, but a more thorough understanding of the basic examination may help, so we offer you our observations.

Anger is probably the most misused emotion of all and that causes the most damage to the system. The four products and poisons of anger are resentment, retaliation, revenge, and repression. We do find that it is necessary to express anger in a healthy manner—not to pretend that it doesn't exist. It is not likely that all our anger, a basic human emotion, will suddenly disappear and that we find ourselves running for sainthood. We don't consider it "wrong" to share how we feel to clear the air, or to keep communication lines open, but we do not want the anger to be extreme and poison us, affecting us negatively.

Nursing anger over long periods of time is called resentment—a feeling which causes us to be irrational, grouchy, and puts a shadow over an otherwise sunny sobriety. Retaliation is a loss of control (punching someone in the mouth); it causes guilt feelings and a low self-image. By trying to even the score with someone, by scheming to make things "just"—the character defect called revenge—we decide we're a better manager than God. And finally there is repression in which we deny anger, turning it inward, sometimes to the point of causing psychosomatic diseases or suicide. All forms of anger have to be dealt with in an honest, open, healthy way.

It seems that all we seek is peace and harmony, yet so much time is wasted on either being angry or trying to avoid the anger of others. It is very important that we come to realize that when people are angry at us, it truly is *their* problem, not ours. If we are sincere in our actions, if we stick to our principles, then other people's anger remains their problem. We don't need to whip ourselves with it. This does not mean, however, that we go around chirping smugly, "That's your problem, not mine," everytime someone is mad at us. What do we do when a friend or loved one has a problem? We offer to help, don't we? So a calm discussion, sharing, and caring, is what seems to work best for us.

Now our own anger. Did you know that you are in business for yourself? It's called the Control Business and the sooner you get out of it, the more at peace with yourself you are going to be. In all honesty, most of us expect people, places, and things to be our way and if they aren't, if we can't control, then POW, we become angry. "If only Mom would wash my jeans right; If only Dad would let me drive the car; Mary should loan me money like a loyal friend; my boss ought to give me a raise." What makes you, or any of us, think we know how others "should" behave or not behave? Nobody we know lately has been nominated to run as an advisor to HP. If we don't like the way people do things, we should try to do it ourselves; if we don't like how people treat us, we find friends who suit us better. In the case of parents, we have home rule Number One: When under their roof, be under their rule, or out in the rain. Because it is so distasteful to be under the control of others, we drop our controls *from* them and amazingly anger is seldom an issue any more. When it is, we pause and say something like, "Guide me, please, in the words I say, in the steps I take, through this day."

The best exercise we know of to get out of the control business is to see one's self in the other's place. The old Indian saying about "not judging another until I have walked a mile in his moccasins" makes a lot of sense to us. This will bring our basic spiritual forces together that will prompt understanding and lessen the animosities. People don't really want to hurt us; they are generally too self-centered for that. They may want to feel good, or protect themselves, or have things go their way, but setting out to hurt us or anger us is not usually their motive. Was it ours?

Guilt or self-blame, is worthless. What good does it do anybody, least of all ourselves, to *feel bad* about mistakes we have made? We need to correct any mistakes or wrongdoings, put an effort forth not to repeat them, but feel bad? That accomplishes nothing. If your grades come back from school and are less than you are capable of achieving, do your parents want you to feel guilty? Probably not. What they want you to do is to get better grades! Shedding guilt leads to a more comfortable sobriety. Even if other people try to induce feelings of guilt in us, we refuse them.

Fear opens the door to worry, doubt, loneliness, self-pity, anxiety, and gray hairs. Worry is only a fear of tomorrow and the where and when. Live in the here and now, remembering that worry weakens and action strengthens. When the time arises you will get what you need. Doubt? Why doubt when you can pray? Loneliness? There is only one reason we know of in the Fellowships for loneliness and that is a person's own choice. If you use, you use alone, if you die, you die alone, but if you want fellowship and love, here we are.

Self-pity? This is the fear of not getting our fair share. The thing to remember here is that if we got our fair share of the trouble we've caused, the water would not be up to our neck, it would be over our heads. So we get off the pity-pot, give thanks that we didn't always get what we deserved, and we show gratitude for what we have.

Anxiety is the fear of the unknown. In our group, we have discovered that the best way of dispelling all fear of the unknown is to develop a straight connection with our Higher Power. We have to clear any doubt of our connection with the Divine Source and that is done through prayer and meditation. Fear of any kind is the enemy to our spiritual development. It hinders healthy relationships, fragmenting us. We correct this fragmentation by helping the still-suffering alcoholic and addict, and that maintains our unity, our purpose, our direction.

Our constructive purpose in relationships is to cultivate positive emotions like love, patience, tolerance, trust, kindness, forgiveness, and many more. The principle of cause and effect here is simple—if you want love, be loving; if you want forgiveness, forgive; if you want friends, act friendly. The best investment we know of in personal relationships is to spend self. When we spend self, the interest from our investment will be at least ten-fold.

If your immediate family is understanding and supportive of your recovery, consider yourself blessed. If they hesitate or actually disapprove of what you are doing, walk softly. Don't struggle with outdated or unthinking attitudes towards your disease. They probably just don't know what's coming down. Parents, grandparents, brothers, sisters, aunts, and uncles may not accept you as an alcoholic or addict because of fears, ignorance, and possibly because of drinking and drug problems of their own.

When a child says he is an alcoholic or an addict, parents often ask themselves, "Where have we gone wrong?" They mistakenly think that alcoholism or drug abuse is a moral question and that it reflects on their ability as parents. In dealing with them and their faulty thinking, we merely relate facts and incidents about our history so they know the basis of our disease. But we don't fight to convince them or anybody that the history is true. They may think that it's not serious enough yet. Ask them gently how serious they want it to get. If they want to know more, suggest that they attend Al-Anon or even that they read this book.

A final word about your family: don't expect trust from them as soon as you get sober. How long did you spend betraying any trust they put in you? Then give them some space—some time to come around. They have to *see* you living your new life for awhile to be convinced it's not just a fad or phase. Keep in mind, our parents weren't *always* wrong, though it was easier for us to think that than to look at ourselves. Give them a chance to be right occasionally. They may change, surprisingly for the better, the longer you stay sober.

When discussing the touchy subject of friendships, there are no rules *per se.* But listen. It is unwise to hang out with old pals (or new ones) if all you have in common is getting high. One of our people says:

> "When I first got sober, I still wanted to hang out with my old friends, so I told them I was an alcoholic and I couldn't drink with them or get high, thinking they would understand. Well, they thought I was crazy and I was! Staying with dopers, I didn't stay straight very long. The only thing I had in common with them was getting loaded."

Another member relates:

> "If you run with snakes, you are going to get bit. Soon after I got sober, I found a friend who lived near me and I could relate to her, probably because she was into drugs. I started spending a lot of my time with her and her friends. Everytime we went out and the pipe was passed around, I would just pass it on, feeling I didn't need to get bothered over some pot fumes. One night the pipe came to me and I took it. I got high that night; I got drunk two days later. I got bit."

Not a lot more needs to be said. However, our experience has shown that building sobriety works better without the added burden of fighting doper friends—in addition to our own insanity.

Now sex. We were going to devote a whole chapter to sex until we realized we needn't give it that much priority or emphasis. Romance and sex relationships are governed by the same principles all our other relationships are governed by. No matter what we *thought* drugs were doing for us regarding people we were sexually attracted to, throwing up, acting like a turkey, or being a show-off appealed only to those who were also throwing up, acting like a turkey, or being a show-off. Sobriety really does work better.

As far as sex goes, there is a saying that we subscribe to, "Sex deepens love and love deepens sex, so physical intimacy transforms everything and playing with it is playing with fire."

A final thought—as powerful a draw as romantic relationships are, they do not come first in our lives. The attention we devote to them is only after meetings, after Program, after twelfth stepping. Sobriety is ever our priority or there won't be anything much left of us to have a relationship with.

Kitt

*At times it got so bad that she wished someone
would murder her to end it all.*

I lived with my grandmother and my mother. My mother worked forty hours
a week and was away a lot, so my grandmother ended up raising me. I was an
only child, pampered and loved by all but somehow that wasn't enough for
me. By the sixth grade at least four mothers had told their children I couldn't
play with them, and I was never sure why. At about that time, I started ditching
school with a girl that nobody cared for. She smoked and had already lost her
virginity. We got caught the second time, and the result was that I lost rapport
with all the teachers and cool kids. My grandmother and mother turned on
me, it seemed, and I began talking back. They became suspicious of letting
me go out at night, accusing me of being evil. I remember feeling helpless and
that I was the victim of injustice.

The next three years were very difficult for me. In the seventh grade, I went
through an awkward stage—trying to make friends but feeling like an
outsider in all the cliques. When a couple of the girls that I hung out with
acquired boy friends, I felt like a third thumb, so after school, I would go home,
wrap up in the television set and not let go of it.

Once during these years I attempted to slit my wrists because I couldn't tell
anybody that no one liked me and that I felt like a Martian. I continued fighting
with my mother and grandmother, simply because they didn't understand. It
seemed like there were two parts of me: the me that had to be home, hiding
cigarettes, feelings, secrets, and the me that was with my friends, longing for
attention, acceptance, and openness.

In the spring of that year, an interesting development took place. I began to
hear talk about a drug called LSD. I saw ''ACID'' carved on the back stairs
and bathrooms at school. I started hearing words like, ''flower child,''
''groovy,'' ''hippy,'' ''love,'' ''peace,'' ''free,'' and ''psychedelic.'' Terribly

curious and awed, a friend and I decided to go to a park because we had heard that a bunch of hippies were there. We sat in a group, smoked joint after joint and drank wine, waiting to see what happened. I wanted to be cool. Someone said to me, "Pay a dollar, buy a pill, and swallow it." Finally I did. After a while, I began to feel the affects. The whole world was churning, buzzing, and moving. Feelings, thoughts, cars, people were coming at me fast and all at the same time. Everything I saw was accentuated by a character I saw in it or by an emotion I felt about it. I passed the night at a girlfriend's—my first night of sneaking away from home. Finally the effects of the drug wore off, and I went home. I felt *so* distant from my family. I wanted to feel warm and loved, but that morning those things were impossible.

Time went on, the drugs went on, and I became convinced that what was taught in school and by the system was valueless, meaningless propaganda and that those who had given way to it were ignorant or had "low awareness." All of my reasoning and rationalizing rendered me helpless in dealing with my emotions. Regardless of how much wisdom I thought I had attained, how much soul searching I had done, how much LSD I took, or how deeply I believed in the philosophies I had formed, I could not reach over the wall of isolation I had built around myself. I could not feel whole and secure. I had already acquired a denial system.

Situations at home reached a no-win point. It had become a cold war. Each of us was hurt, sick, and tired. My mother decided that we would move to our own apartment, away from my grandmother, "so our troubles would be over." Yeah, my mother would let me be free! I had little idea of what she was going through and wasn't interested enough to find out. I wanted her to smoke pot and be a different person. I wanted her to understand about all the groovy things that were going on and all the groovy people that I met. Most of those people, incidently, were men whose prime interest was taking me to bed. When I was not in school, I was running around with an assortment of guys, getting terribly drunk or stoned. As months went by, I took LSD quite a bit by myself and began to wander aimlessly around town. I found that a lot of the kids looked down at me and thought I was weird. I strayed around, trying to belong but nobody was terribly responsive.

That year I accidently overdosed on seconal. Everyone thought it was a suicide attempt, and that convinced me that no one did understand. They must have thought I was screwed up, while I thought I was as right as Jesus.

Life became a nightmare. Among other things, I was suspended from school, went to jail, and was raped by a guy I was partying with. It was awful.

Out of desperation, searching for a way out, I went to live with a friend in another state. My mother decided to let me try that because she couldn't handle me. My friend had a loving family—mother, father, sisters, brothers, family—things I knew nothing about. I could not deal with my inability to respond to them, so I became angry and wrote home for money. Back on the bus I went. After I returned from Missouri, I enrolled in high school, but from the first day I felt isolated, different and alone. All I could think about was getting high. I copped some acid, and after school I called my mother at work and told her I would not be home. I went downtown. Some people picked me up, and not knowing what was wrong, they called the police, who took me to the psych ward. Because I didn't come down, I was transferred to a private mental hospital, and remained there five months, continuing to use drugs and alcohol throughout my stay. Because of my continued drug use, they couldn't really help me, and when I got out I felt even estranged from people.

From there I went to an "attention home." I did get back in high school, but two weeks later, I ditched and got drunk. The superintendent of schools came to tell me I was suspended from all public schools. He said the only one who could help me was Jesus. I thought, "Horseshit."

After running away and getting more loaded, more spaced out, I went back home. I stayed high and drunk through the summer. At the end of summer my mother abandoned me, moving to Maryland, and I don't remember saying goodbye to her. Now I was a ward of the court and was sent to the state hospital. I weighed ninety-five pounds, was anemic, and completely irrational. Once more, I was in a mental institution, again five months. I got kicked out for confessing to setting a fire that I had known nothing about. On departure, I felt more helpless and hopeless. My only solution was to stay loaded.

I went from there to a girl's home. I got into needles and managed to keep myself stoned-out. But I broke all the rules at their house, and again was kicked out. I went to a foster home, and, while there, I went to jail several times for being drunk and disorderly. My tolerance for alcohol had gone down and I blacked out everytime I drank.

Finally I had turned eighteen. I drank champagne on my emancipation day and I was *free*, or so I thought. I started running with some women junkies, clinging to them, having sex with some of the women heroin addicts, seeking the affection and the tenderness that wasn't to be found in our larger world. I started turning tricks for money, for booze, and drugs. In the next years, I got beat up, busted, hitchhiked across country alone, got pregnant, aborted, raped, and several times, detoxed. I set up camp in several cities, trying to put my life together and ending up confessing failure. Sometimes I wished that someone would murder me, just so it would be over. My attempts at finding work started proudly. I went from being a waitress to dancing topless, but I was soon fired because I couldn't function. During those days I went to bed with a lot of people, just wanting to buy some time with them, hating the loneliness. I struggled with my sexuality, hating men and the way they treated me, wondering if I was gay. I was anything but free.

One more time, I committed myself to a mental hospital. Afterwards I went back to the streets. I had tried schools and jobs and love. It was hopeless, I would never be happy; nothing would ever go right. Then I called an alcoholic rehabilitation center, seeking help. I told them I thought I might have a drinking problem, hoping they would do something to help me. I didn't really understand what they told me, but I went to A.A. meetings for a while even though I didn't understand what it was supposed to do for me. I kept drinking and things got worse.

At age twenty-one, after many a quart, fix, and pill, I ran into a woman I had met at an A.A. meeting. She took me to another meeting where they talked about my life being unmanageable and my powerlessness over alcohol. I don't know how much I understood, but I knew for the first time in my life that I sincerely wanted to quit drinking. The next day, I went to an A.A. club. I sat and talked to different people, and one of them suggested I go to a half way house. I did just what they said because I had no fight left in me. Picking up the phone, I called the house. Someone came to give me a ride.

I got to the house during dinner and was introduced to everyone. Through dinner, I held back tears although my hands were sweating and trembling. The next night I went to a meeting and listened to some preachy, square looking guy talk about God. The next day, the woman who had taken me to the first meeting came and gave me a book. She told me to take very good care of myself, saying that I had a disease, and that I must take care of myself as if I had diabetes. She told me not to worry about anything and to stay away from situations that upset me. She talked about her drinking, how sick she had been, and what A.A. had done for her.

I'm not sure how or why, but I went to ninety meetings in ninety days and I started to work the Steps of Alcoholics Anonymous. I was confused and full of fear sometimes. I prayed to a God I wasn't sure existed. At meetings, I said that I was an alcoholic, even though I wasn't sure of that. But something happened that had never happened before. My ears were half open and what all these people were telling me was making sense. I began to look forward to going to meetings.

After several months, I was encouraged to get an apartment, and so I moved out of the half way house. My apartment manager was in A.A.; people from A.A. helped me with food, cigarettes, and money until I could get a job. They gave me phone numbers and told me to call any time.

Somehow, over the months, the Program of Alcoholics Anonymous began to sink in. I started learning and growing again. A lot of my fears fell away. Because I hadn't acquired the willingness to do what the people in A.A. told me, I had a lot of problems and suffered many times. But slowly, meeting after meeting, I learned about my illness. I learned about resentment and fear, although a lot of what was said at meetings confused me. I struggled with the Steps, talking to people, trying to understand what they meant. Listening to people sometimes when I didn't want to, I found out that I was not like people who weren't addicted, that I didn't function the way they did. I struggled with problems like jobs, people, my sexuality, christianity, and my identity. And for every question the people of A.A. had an answer. I found gay A.A. meetings, and slowly I am learning how to find my real feelings. I learned to live one day at a time. I learned how to accept myself as an alcoholic and a human being. I learned about my own self deception and the ways my mind twists the truth. I searched for God, finding it within me. Slowly I became acquainted with a feeling that I had never felt before. Everything was o.k. and I am o.k.

I now experience many things that I had missed for years, and hear and read things that enable me to deal with life on its own terms. Tolerance for myself and for others is something I am learning, and surprisingly, I am learning to love myself. I have found Narcotics Anonymous where I am beginning to learn about drugs from a new stand point.

There is much more for me to learn about all of these things, but I feel that a door has been opened to me. Through God and the fellowship of A.A., I have found a new life. And most significantly, I have found that I never *have* to drink or take drugs again.

LEON

He thought that being strung out on heroin was the worst thing possible, until he became an alcoholic.

My name is Leon, I'm the fourth oldest in a family of seven kids, we are black, and my father and mother are God-fearing people who go to church quite often. In writing this story, I wish I could tell my roots, but the background I have on my family is short, and what I know has a lot to do with alcoholism. My mother's father died of alcoholism, as did his brother who was my great uncle. So did my mother's brother, my uncle Neal.

When I was a kid I used to watch my uncle Neal drink, and I would tell myself that that would never happen to me. On Christmas Day when I was about five years old, I had my first drink of alcohol—a sip of my father's beer. What I most remember is that I didn't like the taste, but I did like the bubbles. As I grew older, I started liking not only the taste of beer but just about any other drink I could get my hands on.

In high school I had a friend named Wade and we would get high everyday during first, second, and third periods. It was then that I started smoking pot and liking it, but it had its drawbacks because my teachers could smell it on my breath. One thing led to another, and in my senior year in high school, I started drinking cold medicine with codeine in it. I remember that every morning at 9:00 I would meet Wade and we would skip class, go down to the drug store, and buy two bottles of Robitussin AC cold medicine.

Buying cold medicine was alright because it didn't smell like alcohol, and when I went home high at night, my mother never knew what was wrong with me. She would ask why I was always so sleepy, and I would tell her, "Hey, Mom, I have to stay up late studying, and besides, I work hard to get money." Because she couldn't smell anything like alcohol, nothing more would be said.

Later, it dawned on me that because I liked both scotch and cough medicine, it might be good to mix the two together. Well, let me tell you, this was great! I found myself being able to do all the things I was never able to do straight. Now don't get me wrong, I couldn't run faster or jump higher, but I sure could talk better and think better and I could fight better than ever before.

The one thing that I thought was just super was that when I drank scotch and cold medicine it turned me into a top running love machine. Sex lasted longer and was much more enjoyable when I was high. Now, I would hear in school about how drugs would make you lazy and hurt your body, but I thought that only happened to weaker people. I worked eight hours a day, went to school for six more, and felt great. Any drugs that could turn me into a sexual giant and marathon man couldn't be all bad. Right? Well, my honeymoon with alcohol and cough syrup lasted right up to Christmas of that year.

On the evening of the Saturday two weeks before Christmas, I was in my favorite bar, drinking shots of scotch with beer chasers, waiting for a friend of mine to bring me a couple bottles of Robitussin. He didn't come, and I was at the point of leaving when he came in. I quickly drank my two bottles of AC then continued drinking scotch. At about 1:00 a.m. I decided it was time to go home, because, for some reason, I wasn't getting high or drunk. About 1:30 I went home to go to bed, and the last thing I remember was sitting on the edge of the bed smoking a cigarette. About 3:00 a.m. I woke up with my bed on fire. I tried to put out the fire without my parents seeing the smoke, but I couldn't. My sister and mother both smelled the smoke and helped me put it out. That was the first time, so I thought, that alcohol and drugs got me in trouble.

About a month later, I was playing with my band at Syracuse University at a frat party, and the guys giving the party were pretty drunk. After the band had played for about an hour, people started throwing beer around at everyone, including the band. After a while it seemed that I was the only one out of the six people in the band that hadn't had beer thrown on him.

Well, everybody seemed to be having fun, and I kept drinking the Tom Collins' that had been made for the band. It was the first time I had ever had Tom Collins' and they tasted pretty good. After about fifteen drinks, I made up my mind that if anyone threw beer on me, he would be very sorry. It just happened that that night I had a cane with me that had a twenty-four inch knife inside it. I was told about the knife on the next day.

At about 1:00 a.m. some guy decided that it was time for me to get a beer bath. Well, when he started to look at me with a big pitcher of beer in his hand,

I told him that he had better not throw that on me. He just smiled, told me to go to hell, and threw it. Then he stood there waiting for me to do something. The first thing I did was wipe the beer off my face. I told my smiling friend, "You just wrote a check with your mouth, and now it is going to be cashed." I grabbed my cane and pulled out the blade. My smiling friend stopped smiling and started running up stairs. I was right behind him as we got to the top of the steps. As I pulled back to hit him with the sword, I felt a hand on my arm. My bass player had caught up to me and he grabbed my arm just as I was starting my down swing; the sword stopped about three inches from the guy's head.

That party was the only time I ever tried to kill anyone in my life. It was also the first blackout I ever had, and as I said, the next day, Dave, the bass player, told me what I had done. After that night of drinking, I told myself, I would never get drunk again, and I would never carry that cane again. But I did go back to alcohol and other drugs.

Three days after my big drunk, I decided that I was going to take more drugs and stay away from the alcohol. At school, I continued to meet Wade, as usual. We had no plans to interrupt our consumption of cough medicine, but there had been a big drug bust in the recent past, and a law was passed that you had to be twenty-one to buy Robitussin—and that you could only get it by a doctor's prescription.

After about two days of no Robitussin, Wade told me about a drug that was just like Robo, only it was more powerful and cost more. He called it "skag." That afternoon was to be my introduction to heroin. I had heard that this was a habit-forming drug and that it was hard to get. Well, it took us about ten minutes after we got out of school to find someone we could cop from.

I was still kind of worried about getting strung-out on drugs, so I asked Wade about heroin's habit-forming effect. Wade's answer to me was, "You only get a habit if you do it every day, not once in a while like we would do." So I said, "Let's do it!" That first day I thought I would never drink again because heroin didn't make me smell like alcohol did. I knew that this was my kind of high.

For about a year I got high on heroin every day either before or after work. It was only by luck that I always made it to work—high or not high. One Friday evening, I took a light overdose of skag and fell asleep on a radiator. I woke up about two hours later with a skin burn about the size of a silver dollar pancake. I worked around coal boilers the next night I went to work, and I told them I had burned my arm on a hot piece of coal at work.

Everybody except me was concerned about my arm. The company doctor said I would have to have a skin graft operation and I did. My employer paid for ninety-eight percent of all doctor bills, gave me sick pay for two weeks, vacation pay for two weeks, plus $350. Every penny went for drugs.

It wasn't long before I got fired. Three months after I lost the job, I got busted for selling drugs and was sent to a drug rehabilitation center for eight months. After getting out of the rehabilitation center, I was busted again for drugs. At that point I told myself no more drugs and started drinking again.

Now, during this time, I had left the state, running from drug charges. My "new" life included alcohol, not other drugs, but my need for alcohol had turned into a twenty-four hour thing. I remember talking with a friend who was an alcoholic, telling him that there wasn't any way in hell that I would let alcohol interfere with my life or job. Yet, it all seemed to be happening. I told my friend Fran that the worst thing that could happen to a man was to be strung-out on heroin. He just laughed and said, "I hope you never become an alcoholic."

I don't know what ever happened to Fran, but he was right. Trying to stop drinking has been the hardest thing I have ever done in my life, even harder than quitting heroin.

After losing about twenty jobs and using every woman I have ever loved because of alcohol, I decided that it was time to get help, but from whom or where I didn't know. The first thing I did was call a hospital. They told me that I would have to stay there from five to fourteen days, something I didn't want to do, so I said no. Next I called an alcohol treatment center, but they asked for money down. They wanted to make a credit check and charge me $3,600. I felt they were just trying to rip me off, and anyway, if I had that kind of money, I would have been out getting drunk instead of wasting my time calling them. The last and only place left I could think of was A.A., so I gave them a call. I talked to a man named George, who came and met me in a laundromat. Later that night he took me to an A.A. meeting, an open speaker's meeting.

At the close of the meeting he told me more about the Twelve Steps of recovery, and said that if I wanted to stop drinking, I could. He went on and told me about his own drinking career. I was impressed but not enough to stop drinking. It took another two years of drinking for me to realize I was slowly dying, just like my Uncle Neal. I had finally become what I never wanted to be, a man like my Uncle Neal. Not that I didn't love that man, I did. Like it or not—my grandfather was a drunk, Uncle Neal was a drunk, now I'm the third generation drunk in my family.

Being at a point where I could no longer endure life, I knew I must stop drinking and taking drugs or kill myself which I did not have the courage to do, thank God. So my next answer was to call A.A. once again. I did that exactly one year and nine days ago. I now have a good job and have decided to go back to school. Family and friends want me to come back home. My father and I have learned how to talk to each other once more.

For the first time in my life I've got something no one can take away from me and that something is me. For this change in my life, I'm grateful to A.A. But I also thank God, for only He could have done what no others were able to do. This is not the place where I have to be, it is the place where I am. The world is not my prison but my home. It is the road I must walk; the walking of it is called life. Because I will walk it only once, it is very important that I should walk it in some way that I can call my own.

7

To Parents, By Parents

"I came to understand that my son could not live by my life experience; he had to have his own."

Elaine

Don't be surprised when you first learn that your child is or may be an alcoholic. As parents, we can't help but be shocked because we honestly believed our child could never become seriously involved with drugs or alcohol at his or her age. Although the truth may be difficult, believe it, accept it. Some of us have noticed that our child has a serious drinking or drug problem long before he or she does. Perhaps the child may have to smoke a joint before school or comes home regularly under the influence. Here is a mother's description of how she learned of her son's problem:

"During my son's high school days, I knew he was drinking beer and smoking pot while he was in a band which practiced and held jam sessions in our basement. My husband and I were concerned, but thought this was a phase of his life, that it was a normal process of experimentation and learning. We thought that he could cope with it, so at first we certainly were not obsessed with it.

"As time went on, it was evident that problems were arising: an accident with his van, a few signs of physical abuse, bruises, black eyes .... I called him at work one day, and was surprised that he was drinking at work, his speech was impaired, thick tongued. I found this very disturbing and began getting upset. We had found out he was drinking at work regularly, also getting drunk nights. I was getting really up-tight! I was so afraid he would have an automobile accident, imagining all sorts of horrible thoughts while sleeplessly tossing at night.

"One night he parked his car, opened the door, and just fell out on the street. We went out to help him in the house. More and more often, we would help him into the house, help him to the bathroom, help him to bed. He began to wet the bed frequently. We would talk to him when he was drunk, and we could see this was useless, only making matters worse. And we didn't understand why."

After discovering the illness, we don't take it lightly, and we don't come down on the kid too harshly. We can inadvertently drive him underground or completely away from home. Be patient, be kind, and seek help. Hard as it may be, we try to understand where our child is and what the problem is. The addictions syndrome is an illness. If the child had leukemia, we would be understanding and we would learn as much as possible about the disease. Alcoholism and addictions unattended can be just as fatal. Attend open A.A. and N.A. meetings as well as Alanon meetings. Listen at these meetings; they will tell you how to work on *your problems* first. Many of us have balked at this. "It's their problem, not mine," many of us have exclaimed. But in reality, it is our problem too—the problem of understanding, patience, guilt, game-playing, and so on. Another parent describes how Alanon was able to help her with her desperation and non-acceptance:

"Needless to say, I became *desperate!* I began going through articles regarding "Alcoholism," which I had clipped from newspapers during the previous year of deepening concern. I found an article very appropriate to our situation regarding an alcohol awareness program being conducted for persons with Driving Under the Influence problems. In desperation, I called the promoter who was very helpful and concerned.

"She suggested I talk to her and attend an Alanon meeting that night. Having no close relationship with alcoholism, I was completely unaware that there was such a group. I was warmly received at the meeting, and I listened to various people express how they were able to cope with the same problems, the same feelings of guilt, fear, and frustration that I was experiencing. It brought just a wee bit of enlightenment, and the strength to accept the fact that perhaps I could be helped. I really thought many times that *I* was going insane!"

In understanding, a certain peace comes. Often we feel a deep pain in knowing what lies ahead and how difficult the road to recovery will be. Sometimes we think ignorance would be bliss, but it is not only the child who is in some isolated trouble—bear in mind, you have a similar problem, too, as a parent. Help yourself to tackle this problem, as you are as much involved as the alcoholic.

We are not recommending, however, that you wallow in self-recrimination saying, "Where did I go wrong?" You probably didn't and if you did, it was so long ago, you couldn't remember—nor, in fact, does it matter. What really matters today is the children's sobriety and your sanity. This disease is not a reflection on you as a parent. If neighbors or the school system ride you with "Do something about that brat of a kid of yours..." or any recriminations like that, explain as gently as possible what you have learned and what you are doing but refuse to accept any blame. A father explains his viewpoint:

"I don't accept the 'fact' that I or my child is to blame. We are all victims of circumstances and do the best we can to cope with the 'injustices' of life. There is good in everything if we look for it. I believe my child has gained great strength of character as well as great insight into himself and life, because of these experiences. What a beautiful happening."

There are feelings of helplessness, we know. Addiction is not a skinned knee that we can put a bandage on. Often our children expect us to "fix" them but we learn to encourage them to seek help from their peers in young A.A. and N.A. groups. It is the best way, although very difficult, to face the fact that we are no longer the "Fixer." A parent explains:

"It was at this point (his beginning recovery) that as a parent I found it most painful. This was mainly because experience told me that I could not be the one to help and advise. A.A. and N.A. would work for him, if I stayed out of it. For me to selfishly impose my role as father or close-friend (which he and I became in this struggle) would have been to complicate things for him. Now, he needed to keep it simple."

Just because you did it your way, will you demand of your child, "I did it my way, so you do it my way"? Allow your child to say, "I did it my way," too. It may be hard to accept that a group of weirdo kids can help when you can't. It is extremely important to let your child attach his signature to his new way of life. Another father shares his experiences in this way:

"When confronted by teenage alcoholism, we were most surprised, but our daughter wanted help. She sought it and we encouraged her. This meant driving her across town to meetings in funny old churches with weird kids (who were their parents?). It meant trusting her and her friends to give her a ride home (could they be trusted?). It meant that she stayed out late (who were these other kids?). It meant having strangers to our home—kids from outside the neighborhood (who were they?). As we learned and grew with our daughter, we learned about her problem. We learned all these kids shared common bonds and helped each other receive a gift in life that neither their parents nor ourselves, no matter what means or status, could ever give—and that gift was SOBRIETY."

The most important thing to do is to show love and understanding. Remember, your child hasn't failed you. Don't ask, "How could you do this to me? .... Embarrass me?" Remember, we deal with a disease, not a moral problem or a "bad seed" character. Blame or punishment will not help. At this age, the young alcoholics and addicts need more patience than punishment. Severe reprimands and physical restraints won't help. Just as the adult alcoholic will hide his bottle from the scolding wife, so will an adolescent alcoholic hide his drinking by doing it at school or behind the neighborhood convenience store.

Also, we have come to know that it is important not to forbid your child from going to A.A. or N.A. meetings as a punishment. There are two reasons for this:

1) Meetings aren't for fun, they are serious therapy. We wouldn't stop a sick child from seeing a physician as a means of punishment.

2) We add to the resentment and animosity by preventing him from talking to maybe the only people who really understand. Our child is not playing an attention game; alcoholism is a serious disease.

But what about the illness? Don't let them use their drinking or drug problem as a cop-out. They may try to con you into extra privileges because they're "sick." In most respects they are just other kids. You and they have the same parent-child relationship as any other family. Use your best judgment to handle other problems.

We would note that your son or daughter needs to face the realities of his or her behavior while still using, just as certainly do he and she need to while sober and clean. If you choose to bail out your child from his involvement with breaking the rules, think very carefully concerning the greater good. Youth is the time for growing up. Let them. Allow your child to face the consequences of his own actions. At times this may mean painfully letting them go to jail or being expelled from school. But it will pay-off in the long run in life experience for your kid. Growing up after forty is more destructive and also destroys the lives of others. None of us wants to see our kids reach senility before reaching maturity!

In summary, be patient and understanding. Sobriety is not instilled by the switch or the strap. They can find sobriety through their peers in A.A. and N.A., through lots of help, and mostly lots of love.

Never confuse your love of the child with your hatred of the disease. Loneliness is a fear we all share. Let your child know he or she is not alone, that they have you, always. No matter what, there is a light waiting for them when they want to come home. And as your child's recovery begins, you may find that you even enjoy sharing this great adventure with him.

Lori

*Her parents helped her pour
her bottles down the drain.*

I wasn't a social drinker. I don't think I ever had a social drink in my life, except possibly when I was about six or seven years old; my father used to let me have sips of his drinks. All through my childhood I was Daddy's Little Girl, but as I grew older, I started hating him more and more. You see, my father was an alcoholic. I didn't like the things he did or said, but most of all he scared me because I could relate to his feelings.

As far back as I can remember, I was always very frustrated. No matter how I tried, I just couldn't fit in anywhere. In school, I was lonely and scared, and around seventh grade, started drinking and smoking. I discovered that when I had something to drink or was loaded I didn't have to look at Lori and her feelings. Because I didn't like Lori, getting away from her was great. Booze gave me strength to be who I wanted to be. Then it started to take more booze to get that feeling, and pot just never was enough.

For me, booze was easiest to get. Because my father was still drinking, we had a bar at home filled with anything you could want. Dope was more difficult to find. I knew the right people, but on an allowance of three dollars a week, it was a little hard, so I found it easy to stick with liquor. I never really thought too much about not having control over my drinking, but time after time, I found myself drunk when I didn't want to be. Even then, I thought I was cool, but I started having blackouts, and I'd make the biggest fool of myself, so I was told. A drunk girl wasn't a very pretty sight, especially when it was me.

I started cutting classes. I wouldn't go a day without cutting a class. Then I started just not going to school at all, or going once a week. When I skipped school, I wasn't off with my friends having a good time. I wasn't with a boy friend. I was home all by myself, drinking and watching TV, drinking until I passed out or until I cried myself to sleep. Booze wasn't fun any more. It ruined every form of relationship with guys, and most of my friends even stopped calling. I would sit in front of the TV with my drink and cry. I hated myself so.

One day I had what I think was an hallucination. I could hear the wind howling outside, and it wouldn't leave me alone; it kept telling me that I was possessed, and that my life would never get any better. Finally I passed out, never so scared in all my life.

I did have one friend whom I thought understood me. One day he called, we talked, and he told me I was an alcoholic. I said that I couldn't be because my dad was, and when he drank, he was violent. When I drank, I was a basket case. He challenged me to see how long I could go without drinking. I went four days, and that fourth day killed me. I had gone to school and it was dragging on as if it would never end. Finally it did, and when I got home, I went straight to my dad's bar. I started crying, and in half an hour I was drunk again. Then a friend walked in; I threw my drink at her (another friend lost!), but she had brought someone with her, and they stayed with me, trying to calm me down.

I didn't want the guy that I made the bet with to find out that I had drunk, but some how he did, and told me the next time I wanted a drink to call him. The next Sunday I woke up wanting a drink. I started over to the bar, but then I remembered: Sunday. My father was in there. I had no more booze in my room, but I felt that I had to have a drink or I would go crazy. The only thing I could do was give my friend a call. I did, and he told me to come over to his house. When I got there, I broke down and cried, shaking all over and not able to stop. He called my parents and told them that I was really upset. They came and picked me up, and when we got home, my mother asked me what was wrong. I wanted so badly to tell her, but I couldn't. Everytime I opened my mouth, I started to cry. So to save me the pain she guessed, and she guessed right! I was an alcoholic, but at the time I only admitted to having a "drinking problem." However, that was a big step. My mother had been going to Alanon, so she already really knew. It wasn't a surprise to her, but it sure was to my father. Then all three of us walked to the bar and poured each bottle down the drain. I thought to myself, "What am I going to do now."

As we continued talking, my mother asked me if I wanted to go to an A.A. meeting. I was so confused I didn't know what to do, so I went.

When we got there, there was a lot of laughing, something I hadn't done in quite awhile. The laughter sounded very nice, but I looked thorugh the room and—fifteen at the time—I didn't see anyone my age, not even within ten years! This made me feel somewhat uncomfortable with the group, but they told me to keep coming back. I honestly don't think I would have, but one of the women offered to bring me, so I began to go with her.

Soon, she became my sponsor. She tried to help me, but in spite of everything, I wasn't ready yet. I wasn't convinced I had the disease. Maybe I did, I said, but I couldn't—or wouldn't—admit it. I wasn't finished trying to kill myself, but I kept coming back because they had something I wanted. They enjoyed life and they treated me as though I belonged. I had finally found somewhere I fitted in and they were willing to help if I only became willing to help myself.

Later the realization hit—I had killed myself a long time ago! Now, I felt that my life had gotten so bad that I was willing to do something about it. The first thing I learned was to call someone when I was down, *before* I took the first drink. Then I learned that calling alone wouldn't keep me clean and sober; I had to find a Higher Power. This was very hard for me, because I believed in Him, but I didn't think He believed in me. I tried to pray, but instead of praying for His will, I was praying for mine, and that's not the way it works.

I learned I had to move aside and let someone else take over my life. I had to pray for His will and be sure my motives weren't selfish or dishonest. Doing this was difficult because all my life I had been selfish, self-centered and very dishonest. So all I could do was pray, "Thy will be done." And then, strange things started to happen. I began feeling good inside after I had said the prayer. I started to pray more often, and His will started to happen. Before I knew it, I was eating my year one cake at the A.A. meeting I felt I didn't "belong" to. I was going to school and going to my classes. I started doing well in school. I met new friends, and best of all, I wasn't drinking.

I began living. I mean *really* living! Before, I merely existed. Today I have true friends, and I didn't have them before.

When I first came into the Program, I resented that everyone else had been allowed more drinking time than I had been, but today I'm glad I was spared from drinking for the past five years.

I still get the "You're too young to be an alcoholic," or the, "I spilled more than you drank," but those remarks don't bother me because now I have the rest of my life to live.

Today, I also realize that age has nothing to do with this disease, and that it truly is a disease. No matter what our age, we all share the same feelings.

I still lie and I'm still self-centered. I still do a lot of things that aren't socially acceptable. But today I'm happy and, most of all, I like Lori—and Lori is sober —and coming from where I've been, that's saying a lot!

Suzi

*She thought her mother **really** hated her,*
so there was no reason to even try
to be "good" any more.

I am writing this story to share with you my experience, strength, and hope as a young recovering alcoholic and drug addict. I was introduced to this Program of recovery in the summer of '71 at age nineteen. Though I was rationalizing at first that I was too young to be a "true" addict, I stuck with the Program until December of '71, when I started truly *living* the Program, and thus began my return to reality. Now I am convinced of the true seriousness and progressiveness of my disease. It is no longer true that "I was too young" or that "I had not gone far enough." Those were the ultimate in rationalizations. I ht bottom at the age of nineteen. That was seven years ago, and I have been free of mood-altering chemicals since.

I come from a large family, almost all of whom drank alcoholically. Today, there are eight of us in the family who are on the road to recovery. Some have not made it. Mom died two years ago of the disease. A sister, five years older, is still not convinced. But some cousins, an aunt, an uncle, and a step-father are all sober in A.A. This in itself is a miracle. All of us do a lot of sharing, giving, and loving. We share a common disease, which doesn't respect any age, color, or economic status. For the gift of my family's and my sobriety, I am truly grateful.

As a daughter of alcoholics, being brought up in an environment of alcoholism, there were many things that I assumed were normal. When people drink they get drunk, forgetting what they do, saying and doing things they would not usually do. I remember everybody sitting around in the morning, drinking coffee or bloody Marys, laughing and saying they were sorry about the night before. On Holidays everybody got drunk—usually fighting, often screaming, yelling, and hitting each other. That was just part of the celebration. Even the kids got to participate one Chirstmas. At the time, I was seven years old and I would give anybody a kiss and a hug for a sip and a dollar. That Christmas, I made nearly $30 and got a buzz on. People told me how cute I was; the liquor was exciting and fun. Early on, I learned how to drink and get away with it, and when the fighting would start, I either hid in my room or joined them, depending on my mood and the amount of alcohol I had drunk.

My mother and father divorced when I was quite young, and the divorce was preceeded by a lot of fighting which would often wake me up. One time, Dad was pulling Mom out of bed by her hair; she was screaming. I cried and hid. Another time Dad took a knife after Mom. My sister gave my brother and me a high heeled shoe, and she took one of Dad's belts. "We have to stop Daddy before he kills Mom!" she yelled. Dad stopped when Mom said, "Please don't kill me in front of the kids." When the fights ended, he would cry or leave, and Mom would always come and hold us, saying, "Daddy just had a little too much to drink." The next day everything was o.k. again.

My mother was a very attractive woman, and she found it very easy to get a job in a cafe-bar, where she ran the kitchen as well as waited on tables. After my father left home, Mom—who loved to party—began to date a lot. As a consequence, she wasn't able to do a lot of work at home, and often, the three of us kids—Tom, Patty, and I—ate at the bar.

I would drink Shirley Temples, and I loved the music and the attention. I was Mommy's little baby girl, the youngest of the three, and got to spend a lot of time with her. Tom and Patty didn't enjoy the bar, so my friends soon became the people in the bar.

After a very short time, Mom was remarried, and we moved to Texas with her and New Husband. I didn't like New Husband much and he didn't like me. After being in Texas a while, he was transferred to Florida, which didn't seem any better than Texas. Mom and he were fighting regularly, and a familiar scene repeated itself night after night. They would go to the beach, dance, drink wine, and come home and fight.

All the while, my sister was growing into a beautiful girl, and I was the chubby little sister that bugged her. I was so jealous of her. When I was ten and she was eighteen, she won a beauty contest. A surfer and a good dancer, she had long blond hair, big blue eyes, and large breasts. Needless to say, she got a lot of attention. Me? I was kind of short and fat, with short brown fuzzy hair, and no breasts. I resented her to the utmost. My brother did well in school, and New Husband really liked him, so I was jealous of my brother also. There I was at the age of ten, full of resentment for all the other members of my family.

When Mom decided to leave New Husband, she packed us all in a station wagon and we started back fo California. I was happy to be going home even though it meant living without a lot of money. No money. It did have a good side. Because of the money situation, my sister was sent to live with a cousin and my brother was sent to an aunt and uncle. That meant that I would be alone with my Mom because I was the youngest, and, at last, get some attention. Little did I know this was going to be the beginning of the end for me. Finding an apartment on the beach, she immediately went to work in a bar, and, with her gone a lot, I did pretty much what I wanted.

Boy, did I feel grown up. After school a bunch of us would go to the beach to drink beer and go swimming. It was at a beach and beer party that year that I experienced my first blackout which began when I downed a quart of Reiner Ale. I was with some friends, but I don't remember much of the rest, just coming home and Mom being very upset. But as always, the next day it was o.k.

Mom got married again. This man was charming, exciting, and gave me attention. When they married, we moved to the Valley and Mom went to work as a checker in a supermarket where my stepfather was a butcher. Tom and Patty came to live with us, and Tom worked in the butcher shop while Patty worked as a carhop at a near-by drive-in. But as nice as I thought the situation was, it didn't last long. My mother filed for divorce and Patty announced that she was pregnant. Because I had so much trouble at home, I decided to move in with her and her baby.

By this time I had already been kicked out of two schools for fighting, and I started hanging around with bikers and lowriders. They were the greatest just because they accepted me. We drank quite a bit and partied, and at one of the parties, for the first time, I made love—kind of. I was with a 30-year-old man and somehow it just happened. I didn't enjoy it and it hurt. I felt dirty and bad. Later, while still living with Patty, there was more trouble, I was arrested, kicked out of school, and I scrambled back to my mother's.

She was going to straighten me up. Why, it was just those people that I was hanging around with that got me in trouble. I was down at the beach again, and still in the eighth grade. I hated it because I felt I didn't fit anymore. The kids were still surfing and drinking beer on the beach. But me, I had been riding bikes and drinking in bars, going out with big people. I can remember often saying on Friday night that I would be home around one or two, then not coming home until Sunday or Monday. Mom would say, "Suzie, you are only thirteen. Do you think it's alright to be staying out all weekend going to bars?"

"I don't get in trouble, do I? Now, why are you so upset?" I would reply. My mother tried everything to stop me. Talking with me, beating me, restricting me. I would say o.k. and continue—many times meaning to stop drinking, but inside, I truly didn't see what was wrong with drinking.

From here on my life gets pretty foggy, as it was at this time that I was introduced to drugs. I used LSD, speed, glue, paint remover, and seconal or any downers. It didn't take long before I was shooting barbs, speed, and heroin, although shooting was something I said I would never do. It seemed that it just happened one night when I was already loaded, and the people I was with told me how really great and fast shooting was. I thought that it wouldn't hurt to try it. I did, and I liked it. And things got worse.

One night Mom got drunk and called me up. "If you're not gone by the time I get there, then I'm going to kill you," she screamed through the phone. So I grabbed two pairs of pants and left, deciding it would be better for both of us.

It was early morning when I started hitchhiking to my friends in the Valley. I had been kicked out of the house before, but this time it was different. I realized that she didn't love me anymore. The Valley was a safe place for me, a place where I knew lots of people and had spent many weekends.

The following Christmas, feeling very alone, hoping she'd ask me to come home, I called her. She sure shot that: "Well, Honey, I hope you have a nice Christmas, I have to go." She hung up, I cried. I was sure she didn't love me anymore. I was just too terrible.

Around New Year's, I got busted again and put in the Hall for a few weeks. When Mom came to court, we both cried and held each other. I said, "I never will do those things again, and I will go to school and everything." At home, my sis told me how sick my Mom was over my being gone. Mom and I talked. I found out she loved me and that she did not remember threatening to kill me because she had been in a blackout at the time, waking up to find me gone. With no good-bye or I-love-you letter, nothing, she was frightened and confused. She had called the police who hadn't been able to find me. After the reconciliation it was great to be home.

But it didn't last long. While I was gone, I had fallen in love with a guy and I kept seeing him after re-joining my mother. Soon forgetting to come home, shooting drugs, and drinking, I was in trouble again. Finally I moved out for the last time, and directly into tragedy.

The boy I was in love with shot himself to death. Desperate, I got mixed up with some people that weren't just amateurs, they played for real. I was arrested for passing funny money and I spent three months in the women's county jail at the age of fifteen. Dope was now my whole life.

After jail, I moved in with a family whose only income was from drug dealing and taking contracts on people. One of the men in the group decided that he was going to make love to me. I said no, so he broke my arm. He was in his forties, had a glass eye and a wooden leg. I told him he would have to kill me and he almost did. Another guy that lived there took me to the hospital. I told the doctor how I fell off a chair, but he wasn't buying it and tried to get me to tell the truth. I knew my life would be in danger if I told, but the doctor didn't. I stuck with my story.

During that time, I recall telling God and my dead grandmother, "If this is what life is all about, then I don't want to be here." I believe God heard me because a friend found me and got me out of there.

Lying about my age, I went to work part-time in a bar, and, of course, I spent my sixteenth birthday in jail for being under the influence. My Mom and new stepfather Bill came and got me out. Sarcastically, my Mom said, "Happy Birthday." Bill lovingly asked how I was. Grateful for his not judging me, I promised, "This will never happen again!"

My efforts were tremendous. I honestly tried, but my best effort was to move in with an older man and play house. For two years I really tried to clean up. I just drank wine, did diet pills, reds, and smoked.

While living with this man, I became pregnant and was aborted four times. The hospital helped with the pain each time by giving me morphine and when I left the hospital, I didn't want to leave the morphine. I no longer wanted to play house. I just wanted to stay stoned.

To achieve this, I moved in with my sister. She and I were going to program our drug-taking. We both got waitress jobs, and had a schedule something like this: at 9 a.m. she would wake me up and give me about four or five whites, and we'd go to work. At 1:30 p.m., I would take three or four seconals to get ready for the bar rush. Then at 4:00 p.m. I would take a couple of reds and whites. At 7:00 p.m. we would get off work and buy a bottle of wine or a six-pack to put us to sleep.

I soon became involved with a man who, I'm sure today, was also quite sick. For the next five months we lived together. When it ended, I weighed around three hundred pounds, had been beaten, was pregnant, and could not laugh, talk, or even respond. I thought I was about to die.

I decided to take a month's vacation and somehow go to Denver. Today, I'm sure that this was God working in my life. My mother called my cousin who lived there and told her that I needed help. She had been in A.A. for four years, and although I hated her, I ended up in Denver anyway. As vague as the visit was, I remember her saying I could do whatever I wanted as long as I did it with A.A. people, and that I was not to have drugs or booze while I was there. I said sure. I knew that what she said didn't include my speed and seconal.

I was there for about three weeks—long enough to have my nineteenth birthday on which she gave me a party. The house was full and people gave me presents, one of which was the Big Book. I remember crying that night because I had never been so happy and felt so loved, but crazily, I felt compelled to go back home. Following my feeling, the next day I rejected everything and went home. I couldn't stay straight. I tried a couple of meetings at the beach, then a friend came over with some dope, and "good-bye, Suzie."

From August to December, I went through the old things: beatings, pregnancy, and thinking I was going to die. My mother got me a one way ticket to Denver and told me, "Don't come back to California." I knew somehow that this was the end. I drank and took as many pills as I possibly could on the plane. I was scared, I was happy, I was confused. All I knew was that those people in A.A. whom I met before would take care of me when I got there. I was finally going to be o.k. It seemed to be only a few hours after my arrival that they put me in a half-way house called "The Hand of Hope." I lived there for two months, but I don't remember a lot about it. I was a real sick little lady. Every night for the first week I watched TV in the living room, and weeks later, I was told that there was no TV in the living room and never had been. I also talked with people who weren't there. I had gone in pregnant but decided not to keep the baby. When they took me to a physician, he asked me questions like, "What year is it?" I answered, "1970." It was 1972. He said, "Who is the President?" I laughed and said, "Kennedy!" I couldn't remember the last ten years! I'm sure if he had had his way I would have been put away, but my cousin said she would be responsible for me. I had the operation.

After the half-way house, I moved in with my cousin. And after all that had happened, I was still not completely convinced that I could not take mind-affecting chemicals. About six months after becoming sober I began having headaches, went to a doctor, and he prescribed librium. I got loaded, and was off and running again. Everything I'd gained through sobriety was gone. I again experienced compulsion. I knew I was going down and could not stop.

Thank God, it was only for twenty-four hours!

Through the grace of God and the help of people in the Program, I was able to start with my new way of life again, and I returned to the only honest position. I accepted that I was totally chemically addicted.

Today I believe that if I can say, "Yes, I need something for my pain," then I probably don't need anything at all. It's surprising how much pain we can take when we turn to God instead of pills.

As the sober days grew into sober months, I soon had another half year. At this time I got into a relationship with a man. Soon I was married and pregnant. Today I look back on my marriage and see that I did it for selfish reasons. Although I did love the man, I really got married because I wanted to have a baby, and I felt the only right way to do that was to be married. The marriage only lasted one year.

My child is two years old now and what a gift! Today I have things I never thought possible for me. I have a good job with the state, a three-bedroom house, people whom I love, and people who love me. I have lost one hundred pounds. I even have been able to get some medical training and that's remarkable for someone who couldn't finish the eighth grade.

My new found freedom is hard to express. I like myself today, even love myself. I have respect for myself and others. I found out that I'm not the stupid, fat, ugly, loud, obnoxious girl that I once thought I was. I'm becoming a beautiful, caring, whole woman who is able to feel, touch, hold, and contribute. I no longer feel empty inside.

I can also promise you the same thing that was promised me—*You don't ever have to get loaded again,* nor do you ever have to be alone and terrified if you make a decision that A.A. and N.A. will be your way of life. If you are like me, you really have nowhere else to go and nothing else to lose.

Good luck, God bless. Hope to see you soon.

Are They All Out To Get Us?

*"Most people are busy enough
not to have to go out looking for trouble;
it's usually dropped in their lap."*
Paul

The National Council on Alcoholism, the American Medical Association, the National Institute on Alcohol Abuse and Alcoholism, and other authorities agree that alcoholism is one of the biggest national health problems today. Millions of dollars are spent on prevention and research, even more is spent cleaning up the symptoms of the disease on the highways, and still more on a multitude of related crimes. Fifty to eighty percent of our country's incarcerated people have lost their freedom because of crimes related to alcohol or drug abuse.

Yet when it comes to applying these statistics to young people and their crimes, ignorance closes the gate on the subject. People look at the offense rather than the alcohol or drug problem. Many a teenage alcoholic has committed a crime, been prosecuted, classified as a delinquent, and thrown into some correction center. Many more chemically dependent teenagers, through constant "troublemaking" have been labled as incorrigible and treated for behavioral problems, when, in fact, their greatest problem is a progressive and incurable disease.

It is understandable that the symptoms of our disease would baffle parents and authorities. Look at the multitude of situations from sticky to tragic we get into: petty theft, burglary, running away from home, sexual offenses, pregnancy, dope dealing, expulsion from school, curfew violations, car wrecks, loitering, manslaughter .... These only scratch the surface of what "troublemaking" we are capable. Although we hold ourselves strictly accountable for any damages caused through our disease, we believe that being committed to institutions for behavioral problems is not the solution to anybody's addiction. The major sufferer from this type of misinformed law making and law enforcement is not as much the erring authority as it is the unhelped alcoholic or addict. The incarcerated kid does his time, takes his punishment which is meant to be treatment, and he is just as confused as everyone else, thinking that he is "bad, branded, and a real screw-up." But we know that no amount of correction or punishment is going to help at all until the real issue is addressed: treatment for the disease of alcoholism.

If you find yourself reading this book from an institution such as a jail, detention home, or workhouse, and do not yet identify with us, we ask you to *carefully* and *honestly* evaluate how you got there. Delinquency or disease? Which is it? For those of you already convinced you share our problem, don't let resentment of the establishment prevent you from starting on the path of recovery. Just maybe your HP has something in mind for you.

In fact, we know that there is such a plan. Do first things first, contact outside members of the Fellowship, begin on the Steps, and your purpose then will become clear. Do not let the vastness of projected outcomes overwhelm you and crumble your foundation. Realize that your Higher Power is ever mindful of you. Paranoia strikes often when one is stoned, and it even continues to haunt a person in the early stages of sobriety. You may be convinced that the police are making a special effort to trail you, using every law to try and get you.

The school system may seem to be constantly hassling you, you think that your employer will fire you with the least excuse, and your family calls you the black sheep. If you think that they are all out to get you, you may be right. Look at it this way. You're no angel; none of us can lay claim to any halos. Upon honest evaluation of our behavior, what do we really expect? Didn't we put ourselves in a position for this to happen because of our driving drunk, ripping people off, having loudmouthed negative attitudes? And, friend, because it took awhile to earn our part reputations, it will take awhile to earn new ones.

If we want to stay clean and sober, we must change our prevailing attitudes of hostility towards the police or anyone who appears to have authority over us. These negative emotions can do nothing but harm us, and the game of "bad ass" will only perpetuate already strained relationships. We no longer need to impress ding-bat friends, be "cool" or prove ourselves to anyone. One of the group recalls:

"I used to love to hassle cops. I was always quite pleased when one was killed. I felt like it was a point for our side. I never got hassled bad by cops, but thought it cool to hate them and anybody else in uniform. They were hypocrites and looked down on me. Well, I thought everyone looked down on me or up to me (depending on the time of day). It was all my paranoia or ego that made me feel this way.''

Often we had developed a closed-minded contempt for teachers, cops, counselors, and other authority figures just on General Principles. They have been accused by us of narrow-mindedness, living back in the stone age,* judging us, being hypocrites, and many more gross and degrading things we won't mention here. Now who is narrow-minded? Who is judging whom? Just because you're a space-case doesn't automatically place others in the stone-age.

In reality, our closed-mindedness has just trapped inside of us what little we know, mainly because we so egotistically think we know it all. One cannot be taught anything new if he already knows it all. We *have* to remain teachable so we can continue to grow. Watch a plant. If it's not growing, it's dying, and we feel this way about our Program. So be open-minded to the suggestions of others, even if they do come from the establishment. Those older people may be able to teach you something, they may not. But in any case, with an open mind, you won't miss any valuable opportunities to keep moving forward. One of the girls put it this way:

"I used to judge all teachers (and adults) as the establishment with which I would have nothing to do. Once I had opened my mind a bit, I found a middle-aged woman whom I could relate to and we became close friends. I opened my mind a little bit more, and I found a teacher who was human and who cared. I am now good friends with that teacher. I found most people are similar to me in many ways. Through opening my eyes, I have found some close friends, and, even more importantly, I have seen that nothing can be more rewarding than an open mind."

A number of teenage alcoholics and addicts have been ostracized by their families and end up in group or foster homes. Families, angry and ashamed, not knowing how to handle these kids have signed their lives away. Such a situation seems sad and unfortunate to us and occurs more often than we would like. Given patience and understanding, reconsiderations may be made along the road of recovery. One thing we can always count on in life, however, is change. *Things do change.* In the meantime, we recall that we are a part of a larger family now. A family with members who will never turn their backs on us, and a family with members who *care.* They really do!

We find that as we get older, this is called experience.

After they stop using, most people find that they are no longer forced to deal with courts, cops, and institutions. If these people continue to attack or judge us after we have regained sobriety, we have nothing but compassion for their mis-guided comments. *They* don't understand, but for heaven's sake, with a little open-mindedness we can and do understand.

Kathy

*Many times her faith wavered before
the storms of fear and despair.*

All my life, I have been a seeker, but five years ago I became a finder. I am an alcoholic and a drug addict; I am also an escapist. As a child, I sought for peace in fantasy worlds; later I quested in the equally unreal world of alcohol and drugs. At first I looked for meaning and happiness, in the end I sought only oblivion. At twenty-five, I acknowledged defeat, I surrendered—and paradoxically began to win! It was at that age that I began to accept the hand of A.A., a hand which guided my way to rebuilding the wreckage of my world. My old self had to be dismantled in order for a new life to be reconstructed. The gifts of that new life are what I was searching for all along: a Higher Power, peace of mind, a purpose in life, a feeling of being whole.

The gifts are all new to me. I cannot remember ever being particularly happy before I found A.A. Even as a child I felt different, alienated from the rest of the world. I dealt with fear and confusion by living in a world of books. My development was lopsided; intellectually I thrived but emotionally I withered. Looking back with the clear vision of hindsight, I see the roots of my unmanageability long before I picked up my first drink. The feeling that there was something "wrong" with me intensified when at age eleven, I was taken out of school because I was "too nervous." Later, I would argue with A.A. that I was different, that my problems went deeper than alcoholism.

At age fourteen, however, I discovered how to bridge the gap between other people and me: alcohol. And I drank alcoholically from the beginning—I drank to change the way I felt, and I could not guarantee my behavior after the first drink. I placed drinking at the top of my priority list and I had problems in my life due to alcohol. I drank as often and as much as I could through high school and my first year of college. At the end of that year I was hospitalized for a "nervous breakdown."

This began a long series of hospitals and psychiatrists, which did little for me except help to keep me alive until I found the Program. I discovered drugs in the first hospital (administered by doctors) and quickly opted for their effect as opposed to using alcohol. Considered psychotic at that time, I was given shock treatments and spent the next eight months recovering in a hospital. From this experience I gained almost nothing but a firm belief in my insanity, for which state of mind I took no responsibility whatsoever. Quite the contrary; I felt it was something visited upon me by a cruel fate over which I had absolutely no control.

Not knowing the true nature of my disease, I suffered a great deal of mental anguish in the hospitals. There were suicide attempts, padded seclusion rooms, and the uncontrollable screaming fits followed by blackouts. There was the torment of teetering on the edge of reality, knowing it might collapse at any moment, but being totally powerless to prevent it. Through all these bleak days no one ever hinted that I might be an alcoholic and drug abuser.

Perhaps this was because I was so young, but probably because I was never very honest about my chemical intake. How could I expect anyone to help me when I didn't even consider that a problem? I really believed I *needed* drugs and alcohol to function. It was as though something was missing in me that was present in other people, and I required mind-altering chemicals to bring me up to the same level. I feverishly sought the "right combination" in uppers, downers, psychedelics, and alcohol. I dropped out of colleges and jobs to pursue my research.

I moved to San Francisco to "find myself" and to be where the action was. Once there, I proceeded to immerse myself in it and the action I found all took me to the bottom. I dived headfirst into the drug scene and used everything I could get my hands on, including hard drugs. There was no pretense anymore; the objective was to stay stoned and as far *out* of reality as possible. I knew I was on a self-destructive course and didn't care; life had become too painful to face without a chemical buffer.

I became willing to go to greater lengths for my drugs: lying, stealing (even from friends), trading my body for drugs, making porno flicks—nothing mattered except staying high. Sometimes I switched drugs in an effort to find peace and I grew to be like a chameleon, changing my personality to fit whichever people and drugs I was around.

The hospitalizations occurred at closer intervals, and I could not hold a job. I was running out of family and friends who would tolerate me, but most of all, I was running out of time. I felt like a leaf on the wind with absolutely no control over my life. My typical pattern was to wander down the street and wait for someone to take me home with them for a few days or a few weeks—it didn't really matter. A miscarriage and surgery for a malignancy merely provided excuses to drink and use more drugs. I wanted to die, for death seemed to promise peace. But I even failed at that. My life continued to deteriorate rapidly. I used everything and everyone at my disposal to keep a steady supply of drugs. When I wound up in jail I knew my chances were running out, but I was trapped in the wasteland of addiction.

After jail, I was put on a methadone program and stayed on that for about a year. And then, an incident occurred that finally broke my pride. I allowed another girl to beat my head against the floor without resisting because I was afraid—afraid I wouldn't get my methadone if I fought back. Feeling that I was stripped of the last vestige of humanity at that point, I realized I would do anything for drugs. Something snapped inside and I became willing to go into a hospital to withdraw, my tenth and last time.

That began the climb upward, although it took me another year to achieve sobriety of any length. I overdosed on the way to that hospital and sometimes I look back and I think I was reborn then. The next few months were an ordeal because I was very ill physically, mentally, and spiritually. But something was different. I stayed in what at times seemed to be a living hell; I did not run and it was during these times that I also felt the fleeting presence of a Higher Power. The unmanageability of my life was unmistakable, but I did not know what to do about it. I could no longer exist the way I was and, yet, I could not conceive of a life without alcohol and drugs.

While waiting to be prosecuted for some hot checks, I entered a half-way house. I thought I might be sent to prison but was devoid of all resistance. I had finally reached that bottom which is necessary for recovery. I was completely willing to let someone or something else run my life.

Living in that half-way house was the turning point in my life. There I received the necessary three-fold healing for my disease. I had known of A.A. before, but this was the first time I understood and accepted it. And the program was transmitted not through words or literature but through the attitudes of the people who lived it. I desperately wanted that happiness and peace, that special kind of light which shone in their eyes. I was starving spiritually and they loved me back to health. Through these women expressing a Higher Power, I came to believe in God.

Many times my faith wavered before the storms of fear and despair. At first, paralyzed by depression, I sat in the same chair for hours, unable to speak. I could not read, drive a car, or do other simple things for a while. Even casual conversation terrified me. I doubted the Program would work for *me* (after all, I was different!).

But gradually I learned some basic lessons: *Live one day at a time; Sobriety first and all else will work out; Pray, whether you believe or not;* and, *Substitute people for drugs and alcohol.* And my life did begin mending. At twenty-five I was learning how to live for the first time.

A year went by before I could accept and practice the first three Steps of this Program. By that time I was fully convinced that I was indeed powerless and my only hope lay in turning everything over to a Higher Power. Very simply, this meant going to meetings, staying sober, and working the Twelve Steps.

Since then a miracle of rebirth has happened in my life. Now I am thirty years of age, I have four years of sobriety, and I feel free for the first time in my life. I have more sanity today than ever before and finally I am beginning to feel at home in the world. The emotional turmoil which years of therapy did not quell is dissolving through daily application of the principles of this Program. A few bricks at a time, the walls of fear and isolation are being torn down. And each day I awaken a little more to the reality of a loving Higher Power.

I suppose I will always be a seeker, but now I have the map provided by this Program and all the power I will ever need. And the treasures I'm finding are love, joy, hope—things that cannot be taken away as long as I remember their Source.

John

*He writes his story from prison,
yet he is free!*

Today finds me happy and free—in prison! How can anyone be happy and free in prison? Maybe he's institutionalized. Well, my friend, I am not institutionalized. Instead I look forward to being paroled. This positive attitude has taken me eight years to find, and I am happy and free today because of a Higher Power I found in A.A. This Higher Power, whom I prefer to call God is not some God who punishes people by throwing them in a Lake of Fire. My God loves me. When I make a mistake, He is willing to forgive me, and show me the right way. My God is perfect, but He does not expect me to be.

Since I have found this Higher Power, my life has been wonderful. My attitudes toward people and about things have changed as I look forward to living each day. It is as if He made me a whole new person. As with anything new, it took some getting used to, and each new day was a challenge. I was sober, and I liked it! I was not afraid! My memory was getting better! How could this be? What was happening to me? How long would all this last? I didn't care; I only wanted to enjoy this life as long as I could. For a time, I would stop and wonder if I had really changed. Yes, I did, and it is wonderful to be alive, to be able to wake up in the morning without my hands shaking or my stomach knotted up. I feel great, everything is "zip-a-dee-do-da."

The amazing thing about it all is that I have not had the urge to have a drink in almost a year.

Since I have been in A.A., I have learned about honesty with others and how to be honest with myself. I used to think I was both, but actually it had been so long since I had told the whole truth, I could not carry on a conversation without telling a lie, and changing that was hard. I had to start slowly into a story, watching what I said. When I noticed that I was lying, the story would go to pieces. Having caught myself lying, I would tell the person I was talking to about the lie. Then I would backtrack in my story and try to tell it right. This would really freak some people out, but it sure helped me a lot.

As I write this, I have been sober a little over a year. My sobriety all started with a desire to stop drinking. I mean an honest desire to stop. Not the kind of desire that asks, "What do I get if I quit?" but rather, the kind of desire that says, "I'll take whatever comes along if I don't have to go back to that kind of living." I think it's what is called being humble.

I would like to tell you what it took to get me humble. I started drinking and taking drugs in '68, when I was in the Army. By the time '69 rolled around I had tried every drug I would ever experience. The only drug I have never tried is heroin, and the reason was my fear of getting hooked. That may sound strange because I was hooked on everything else, but you see, I never considered myself hooked on anything except cigarettes. Just because I was always taking some drug, and never in moderation, didn't mean I was hooked. It is a shame how badly we deceive ourselves. Everything I did, wherever I went, booze and drugs were included. They were the power in my life. They meant everything to me. I could not imagine life without them. They *were* my life.

My companions since '68 were resentment, despair, jealousy, hatred, remorse, agony, defeat, and fear. They were always with me, wherever I went. Many times I tried to run away to different states, but my companions always found me, haunting me till I ran away again. I would fool myself, saying, "I won't feel all those awful things if I move somewhere else." Instead they always came along, and they seemed to get worse.

I moved to San Jose in '71, and there I met a young lady. Just like a movie, we had everything in common—our lives matched. She moved into my apartment, and it did not take me long to find out she had a script for phenobarbital. "Great, can you shoot these up?" I asked. She just smiled, handed me five and said, "Let's have a contest, o.k.?"

"Sure," I answered, "you make the rules!"

"We'll each start off with five tabs apiece, then one every five minutes."

"Sounds fine to me!"

Each tablet was one hundred milligrams. Nine tabs and three days later, I crawled out of bed. Ken, a good friend of mine, heard me in the bedroom and opened the door. The first thing he said was, "Glad you made it, want to get high?" I only looked at him. At that exact moment I did not know who he was, or where I was. It took me about an hour to start to get it together. After about two hours, it was possible to make some sense out of what I was mumbling.

Ken told me how much time had passed and what had happened to my girl friend. He had come over to sell some drugs, and when he entered the driveway, he nearly ran over her.

Jumping out of the car to see if she was alive, he turned her over and she barely got these words out, "Tell him I won. I ate twenty-two." Ken asked her what she was talking about, but she passed out. He found the empty bottle of phenobarbital in her hand. He took her to the hospital. At the hospital it dawned on him I might be OD'ed back at my apartment.

Returning to my apartment, he found me flaked out on the bed. Ken said he would have taken me to the hospital, but I'd told him how many tabs I ate. During the three days he stayed with me, all I recall is two bits of memory: crawling from bed to the bathroom and the song "Stairway to Heaven" by Led Zeppelin playing in the background. I do know I never have been so close to death. But, next day I was back to shooting speed, smoking pot, and my bottle was close at hand.

About a month later I bought one hundred hits of acid. The guy who sold them to me told me they were four-way hits. Well, I had eaten a lot of acid before, and figured my tolerance was extra high, so I ate a whole tab. About one hour later I was holding the top of my head saying, "I can't get any higher." It was a good thing I kept some thorazine around or I would have flipped out.

I could run stories like these all day. I was always taking more than enough.

My whole world came crashing down around my ears in the fall of '73. I was arrested for selling marijuana and I was sure the D.A. had me this time. My public defender told me it did not look good at all because the D.A. was talking about two to ten years in the penitentiary. Pending trial, I was released from jail, and since I did not have any failures to appear in court, the Judge granted me a personal recognizance bond. I hitch-hiked to my apartment, proceeded to get drunk, and stayed that way for three days. I appeared in court and the Judge granted me a thirty day continuance, and my public defender suggested I go to live in a half-way house for alcoholics. Since my money was running low and the rent was due, it sounded like a good idea to me. Little did I know how much this half-way house was going to influence my life. There, for the first time in my life, I heard people say that booze was causing them trouble. I never knew people like that existed. Unlike them, there was no way I would admit I was powerless over alcohol. To say my life was unmanageable, that was absurd! How could anyone say that? I came to the conclusion that these people were being brainwashed. I got up to go outside for a breath of fresh air, but once outside, I went directly to the liquor store and bought a tall can of beer. While I drank my beer, I thought about what they had said. Maybe, just maybe, I was like them. NO! NEVER! "Remember," I told myself, "these people are being brainwashed." I continued to drink my beer.

When I returned to the house, chewing gum and smoking a cigarette, I walked into an A.A. meeting. That is one experience I do not wish to repeat. I felt two inches tall as I listened to each one tell how their lives had been ruined by alcohol. As I listened, I kept hearing people saying things which sounded like events from my life. When the meeting was over, I went to bed, but, tossing and turning, I did not get much sleep that night. The next day I wanted a drink so bad I could hardly control it. The day dragged on, and I had to do something, so I talked and drank coffee. During that day I learned that alcohol was a drug, and that you could get hooked. I learned there were periodic drinkers—of course I was not one of those. It did not take me long to see how much like these people I was.

As my court date drew closer, I tried to find people who would go to court with me. I needed all the help I could get, only I was looking for help in the wrong places, in the wrong ways.

I'll never forget my day in court. Holding a bible in my hand, I was the biggest hypocrite in town, but luck was with me, and the Judge granted me probation.

Two months after this I was married because I figured marriage would settle me down. I stopped going to A.A. meetings and picked up the bottle again. A year later my marriage was on the rocks.

We separated and I went back to A.A. Then things began to go pretty good till she told me she wanted a divorce. I told my sponsor in A.A., "I can not understand it. Here I am, giving up drinking so we could be together. Now she wants a divorce." He told me to get hold of myself, not to try to please my wife, but to please myself. This did not make sense to me, so I got a new sponsor and cried on his shoulder. He told me the same thing. He also asked me if beating myself with a whip called pity felt good. Well, I had had enough of his smart comments so off to the bar I went. I learned a lot from these two sponsors, but not at that time. Although what they told me was true, I was not willing to face up to the real me. My final drunk lasted almost a year and a half. I was haunted by my old companions of resentment, despair, jealousy, hatred, remorse, agony, defeat, and fear. And this time, they were unrelenting. I did not know what to do. So I drank more, then drank even more, hoping for pride, self-esteem, and a whole host of other disguises from the bottle. I was desperate. My money ran out, I did not have a job, and my car was repossessed. Everything was a mess, including me. I drank more, and I had no one to turn to. A.A. was still there, but my disguises kept me from opening the door.

"All I needed was money," I told myself. A friend suggested an armed robbery, and I was so bad off, so drunk, it sounded like a good idea. It was crazy, and deep inside I knew we would get caught. To tell the truth, I didn't care anymore. I told my friend that if something went wrong, to give up. "Don't shoot any one . . . ." Murder was too heavy a crime. He carried the gun, and in the store, he didn't even point it at any one. As chance would have it, some customers drove in just as the register opened.

At that moment I had two packs of cigarettes in my hand, and as we turned to leave, I returned one pack to the counter. Neither one of us really wanted to rob that store. I am not backing out of my guilt—just saying we were both confused and didn't want to chicken out in the other's eyes. We made off with one pack of cigarettes. When the police questioned me, all I would say was, "Send me somewhere, so I can get help and re-build my life." Those officers must have had great patience.

I had a different public defender this time. When we first met he leveled with me. He told me that with thirteen arrests but only two convictions, I had a good chance for a reduced sentence. My arrests amounted to three traffic and seven drug related, with one armed robbery, and one for being in a disturbance outside a bar. The D.A. told me at first he was going to make an example of me and give me five to forty years in Canyon City. The Judge told me I had had enough breaks, but he was giving me one more, so my sentence was "indefinite to eight years in the reformatory." I know my Higher Power was watching over me this time.

When I first came to the State Reformatory, I knew I had problems, but the counselors couldn't do anything until I told them, "I have a problem." They have all helped me see that in order for me to make it, I must be honest. I found out that I must be humble and listen closely for my Higher Power's still, small voice within, and I also must watch my feelings in order not to let them run away with me. Even after over a year sober, I still struggle with trying to control my parole plans. Patience helps, and patience is help for many problems along this road of freedom from alcohol and drugs.

I have a sponsor I like. He is not here so I can cry on his shoulder, but he is here to share his experience. I am here to listen and talk over what is going on inside me. When I started the Fourth Step, "Made a searching and fearless moral inventory of ourselves," I was frightened as I started to see a lot of crazy behavior. At this point, I realized my life was really unmanageable; it was full of events that *I* had made a mess of. Now, improvement is not a matter of being a better manager, but rather of letting go and letting God. So before I could go on to Step Five, I had to backtrack to Steps One, Two, and Three. And that is what I mostly work on these days. Each day I go to God asking Him to guide me, thanking Him for hearing me, and telling Him any special things I may have on my mind. Life is really neat now. I am twenty-six years old and still have a lot of life ahead of me. It all began with an honest desire to quit using drugs.

Sobriety is a great way of life. I am looking forward to getting back to the streets. I don't want to get back into alcohol again, but I would not trade this experience for all the money in the world. No one can buy what I learned here, and I learned through what I experienced. For that I am grateful.

Yes, But . . .

"When we isolate ourselves . . .
When we become the exception . . .
When we are convinced that we are different . . .
We die . . . ."

Cindy

Whether you think you are in the same class as the people in this book is your decision. If you believe there still is a good time waiting for you in a bottle, a fix, or a bag—no one can stop you. We might point out that our Program will survive without you, but you may not survive without our Program. One thing we are all clever at is excuses. Having lied to ourselves for a long time makes it difficult now to recognize the truth. When you say, "Well, I identify with a lot of what you are saying and I think I might have the addictions syndrome, BUT I haven't had DT's, or been in jail, or lost a wife, or written a bad check," just attach YET after it. We hope you are not too far gone to realize the progressive character of the disease—it reminds us of a line in a song, "You can check out anytime you want, but you can never leave."

Our explanation of the Twelve Steps and other suggestions may not necessarily be understandable options to you at this time, and frequently they sound bizarre in relationship to our disease, but we have turned into spiritually pragmatic people. Whatever works, works. Even though we cannot see how the Twelve Steps will arrest our disease, we begin by explaining the Steps as ways of working to remove any mental or functional barriers to recovery, and judge the results later. Through the processes of sharing and caring you may be able to relate to the Program. Measure the value in your life *after* the application. If, thinking yourself different, you look away before trying, you run the risk of missing the best, beautiful life that can only be lived through a spiritual program

We have attempted in this book to share our model of sobriety with you in the hope that you will face the light, thus allowing the shadows to fall behind. We would like to be totally optimistic in our approach and say, "You have it made! You are out of the darkness forever." Unfortunately, we know that more of us die from the disease than ever recover from it. But reading this far shows an amount of willingness on your part, and we can truthfully say that for the willing, the chances of recovery are excellent, providing you avoid the traps that have ensnared far too many of us. For simplicity's sake, we have labeled these the "Yes, but . . ." traps and hope that you review them without saying: "Yes, but . . . ."

Trap number one: Yes, but there are times I have to take drugs.

In A.A. we have been told that alcohol is "cunning, baffling, and powerful" and for us that applies to all mind-affecting chemicals. Our disease beckons us in many subtle ways—we get headaches, toothaches, allergies, sleeplessness, develop the "crazies," coughs, and all kinds of psychosomatic and/or real physical complications with which we con ourselves and our physicians into believing we need pills. The con game is the most dangerous of all.

This is not to say that one takes nothing if severely injured or is in a life-threatening situation. Our purpose is to live; the reason we abstain is to stay alive. The value isn't *not-to-use;* the value is *life.* So if, under life-threatening circumstances, a doctor determines that we *need* medication to live, then life takes the priority. We ask for the protection of our Higher Power and accept the situation. Fortunately, it is only *very* rarely that any of us would be in that kind of a situation.

Realize, though, that rationalization can lurk behind every thought. Our disease can influence our mind to extraordinary limits causing us to unrealistically justify taking mind-affecting chemicals. Consider this: you have a broken toe and say, "I can't live with this pain!" Nonsense. Of course you can; you will surprise yourself at just how much you can bear without the aid of chemicals. In fact, as soon as your head *knows* you are not going to take pills, the pain will lessen immediately.

The suggestion most of us follow is this: if any suffering is *so* tremendous that we need medication, then we need to be in the hospital under our physician's care. *Never* prescribe for yourself.

Trap number two: Yes, but what will I tell my friends?

A group member answers this:
"I had a lot of fear when I quit getting loaded because that's all I ever did with my friends. I was afraid they would think I was a turkey. So I had to decide which was more important: my life and sanity or what people thought of me. If they were true friends, they would want only the best for me. I soon found that at that time I had very few friends."
Peer pressure? You don't have to get high for *any* sucker who comes along.

Trap number three: Yes, but why me?

This is an interesting snare catching people who go out and get loaded because they resent the fact that they have this disease! It is similar to asking oneself, "Why do I have red hair, why am I left-handed, double jointed, born in Kansas, one sex or the other," or the classic, "Why am I alive?" These questions are basically unanswerable, or, at the most, the answers are *extremely subjective. Our suggestion: Live first, philosophize later.*

Trap number four: Yes, but I'll never have any fun any more!

Believe us, living life to its fullest is much more fun and exciting than any fogged-up, drug-distorted life we led in the past. Our gatherings are marked by laughter, love, sharing, and caring. One of our group says:
"In my first six months of sobriety, I went to more of the places I had talked of going but had never gotten around to. I met more people than I had met in the last two years of using. I did more exciting things than I had ever imagined possible with my old way of thinking. And, amazingly, I remember them all!"
Do you think you could be bored with the spare time you might have? Let us assure you, *there won't be* any spare time. In between school and/or work and meetings, you will be taking your Steps, talking to your sponsor, and twelfth stepping. Then there are conventions, regionals, round-ups, parties, and other A.A. and N.A. group activities to choose form. You also have a responsibility to your home group: business meetings, clean-up, refreshments, and possibly GSO work. With your new interest in life, you undoubtedly

will start new projects or hobbies. You may even find yourself in church on Sunday morning! Frankly, if you're anything like us, you'll be lucky to squeeze in three decent meals and eight hours sleep in any given day.

Trap number five: Yes, but I'll never be as perfect as the rest of you seem to be.

Hold on a moment! Perfection is not our goal, nor our status. No, we have our fair share of problems; we just work on them all the time. One of the girls put it this way:

"I was constantly beating myself over the head when I was drinking for not living up to my morals and values. I thought this would stop once I worked the Steps, but it didn't. Finally my sponsor had me take a close look at where I had set my morals and values. I found they were close to perfect and I was far from perfect. So, of course, I couldn't live up to them. I had to set them where they were in my reach. They do change to keep up with my growing, but beating myself because of failure will only get me stoned."

Trap number six: Yes, but I need more help than this.

That may be true, but if you're not clean and sober, any therapy you try will be ineffective, mainly, because of your dishonesty. You may not even intend to lie, but in a drugged-up state, you won't even know the truth. We find it is best not to delve into any therapies until one has worked the Twelve Steps and has a firm foundation in sobriety. A member relates her story:

"At three months sobriety, I decided I needed more help than I was getting in A.A. So I got involved with some group therapy with a therapist who was a member of A.A. We met once a week and after each group I would hurt and be in tremendous emotional turmoil. I did not have the tools to deal with all of the awareness I would gain. At that time, I didn't even know how to stay sober much less how to face all that subconscious crap. The only way I could learn to apply the principles of the Twelve Steps was to pour all my energy into them, not "therapy." I started really getting well after dropping therapy and concentrating on my program."

Treatment centers for the disease use a number of techniques to get you in touch with feelings and basic dishonesties—this is fine as long as it leads you into the Program. If you find it *absolutely necessary* to go into or continue therapy (for sometimes it is necessary), then remember that our recovery program comes first. When any conflicts between the therapy and the Program emerge, the therapy loses. With these suggestions in mind, we know you can benefit from the aid of many professionals.

Although people say, "experience is the best teacher," in our case mistakes can be fatal. Learn from our experience, *please.* This is no time to be fooling around, especially when living and dying are the alternatives.

Clearly, expectations and attitudes are important in determining the quality and joy of our recovery program. One has to value being straight, but that takes time and discipline. Are you going to expect the peace of mind and growth of three years sobriety in three days? Are you going to start a program riddled with bitterness and closed-mindedness, grumbling all the while, "Those damn meetings, those funky kids."? If so, we can predict the outcome. Unrealistic expectations will cause negative attitudes, and a negative attitude only generates negative results.

We have a personal responsibility for our feelings and outlook on life. People, places, things, and ideas do not make us act like or feel anything. To say "He made me mad" or "It ruined my day" smacks of dishonesty. "I made me mad," or I ruined my day" says it better, and if I did it, then I can change it. This program has given us a choice. When we choose to feel bad, then that is our decision, but we also have the choice to feel good or at least deal with our feelings in a positive way. Unhappy with sobriety? Look within. The answer lies at your own front door.

You can go beyond the limiting, unhappy beliefs of "inadequacy," "it can't work," "who cares?" "where does it lead?" and that type of bullshit. We all have to keep growing and learning. "More will be revealed to you and to us" is an A.A. phrase our group has clung to. Even these words are not a final belief structure; they are a continuous, *open-ended* process. Likewise, as more knowledge is gained, committees will be formed to update this book. We never want to be trapped in the prison of closed-mindedness or ridgidity—it reminds us too much of our disease.

Not that we don't have phases of skepticism and doubt; we do. However, they are only phases, and given time, they do pass. What really grabs our attention and strengthens our faith is the thousands of recovering young people today. The glow on their faces, the repaired lives, the united families, and the laughter that echoes from church basements, private homes, or other meeting places. We have discovered the "secrets" to living a happy, full life. Not problem free, perhaps, but what were once stumbling blocks have now become stepping stones.

There are no limits to the choices before you now. At our age, the opportunities are infinite. Our chosen boundary is found in a loving God, as you understand Him, and that means living by principle and knowing that all power comes from the One Source. In closing, we wish you well, hope that our paths cross, and leave you with our motto: "Love God and do what you want," because, friend, you have a lot of life to live.

Phil

*Because of his involvement with Alateen and A.A.,
he thought he had been brainwashed into thinking
he had a problem.*

I was twelve the first time I got drunk. I went to a party with my friends and had a good time. I didn't like puking all over the hostess' stereo, or sleeping it off in her brother's bed, or hitchhiking the wrong way home, but for some reason, I remember having a good time even though I blacked out.

My Dad is an alcoholic, and he began to go to A.A. the year I was born, but he didn't stay for long. He continued to drink, and it was ten years before he went back and got sober.

I am the youngest of five kids, and I got a lot of attention from my family while growing up. I don't know how my father's drinking affected me inside but I do remember some outside incidents. My family moved around quite a bit, and times got bad for us as my Dad got sicker with alcoholism. We lived in many different houses and motels, and I was transferred from school to school. The miracle of my Dad's sobriety and the restoration of our family is a story in itself. This story is mine and it is about the miracle of my sobriety.

I started drinking a couple of years after my Dad quit. Hanging out with the "neat" people in my school, and becoming a good member-in-standing of this clique made me feel neat, also. I guess I thought that if I hung out with cool people, that would make me cool. I went from boring weekends of "messing around" to weekends with parties to go to, friends to chase after, and women to try my luck with. Nobody was really into grass at that time, just drinking and popping No-Doz. I didn't want any part of the pills, but I would drink a beer now and then.

I didn't start smoking grass until about six months after my first party, and when I did, I found a new love. Getting high was so much nicer than drinking. I didn't get sick or dizzy, and I really liked that. I smoked about three or four days of the week and when my friends started dropping acid, I would pretend to take it so they wouldn't think I was a chicken. I faked tripping all night long, and my parents busted me after about a year of this. For some reason, they really freaked out when they found out I was smoking grass. There was such a ruckus that I was afraid my mother wouldn't love me if I kept on, so I decided to quit getting high.

Being straight didn't last long. I knew dope would lead me back to the same old trouble, but it was o.k. to drink. Standing in front of the drug store, we would get people to buy booze for us. We'd get very drunk and sneak home.

It wasn't long after I started high school that I started getting high on grass again. I'll never forget the feeling I had getting stoned after being without it for four months. It was great, I loved it. I got off good, and I never wanted to come down again, and I spent the next year trying to accomplish that. I didn't see it at the time but my friends changed to people who got loaded as much as or more than I did. I really looked up to people who did a lot of different drugs and I wanted to be like them. I got into LSD, speed, and drinking. My school ambitions were gradually laid aside and replaced by the extracurricular activity I had: getting loaded. Inside, I was beginning to change a lot. I worried about getting loaded so much, but I didn't know what else to do. I didn't want to get high so often but I didn't think I had a choice. I was seriously starting to think that I might be going crazy, and wondered if smoking was as harmful as drinking. Pot doesn't hurt me, I decided.

From the paper route I had, I used the money to buy dope. One month there was a little trouble when I had spent too much money on dope and ran about sixty dollars short in paying my paper bill. With no way to raise the money, needless to say, I was worried because I had nothing to show for all the money I had made the past year. I was afraid my parents would catch on to the fact that I was spending it all on drugs and booze. But that night, I went out to collect my money from the subscribers, and pretended to have been robbed in order to collect insurance money to pay my bill. I hit my head on the pavement to raise a lump and had a friend punch me in the mouth. I went home crying, telling the family that I had been robbed. They called the police and I was taken to the hospital. As it ended up, I had fractured my own skull and spent the next three days in intensive care.

When I got out of the hospital, I told myself to lay off getting high because it was getting me into trouble. Only two days later I dropped some acid and began to hate myself for not having any will power. Steadily becoming apathetic about everything, I made plans to quit school and run away to

Detroit with two of my friends. No more hassle with parents or school. I would be free! No more hassles with anyone.

Two weeks before I was going to go to Detroit, I told my parents I was in a bad way and needed help. I wanted out of the mess I had created. At least, I thought I really wanted to change, to do something other than get loaded all the time. My Dad suggested Alateen, an offshoot program of A.A., for children of alcoholics. I had heard of Alateen before, and, although it isn't for people with drug problems, I thought I'd give it a try. I started going to meetings once a week, quit hanging out with my old friends, and told them I quit getting high because it was screwing me up. I didn't see much of my getting-high-friends after that, but, in time, I made new friends in Alateen.

I stopped taking drugs and started putting a lot of energy into the Alateen program. As I changed, the hatred was turning into self-respect and I started to grow as a person after such a long time of standing still. I began to believe in God again and saw Him working in my life, but I had a big fear of becoming a "Jesus freak."

Through Alateen, I went to clubs and schools, telling them my story about how I was screwed up and that Alateen helped straighten me out. I really felt like somebody again.

I had not made any kind of decision to stop drinking, I just didn't drink very often. Keeping in mind that I couldn't take drugs or I would wind up right where I was before, I drank because I didn't have a problem with alcohol. I felt lucky. I had learned so much about the disease of alcoholism, I could never have a drinking problem. I would just quit if I saw any problem.

During my last year of high school, I started drinking more, but it never got as bad as the dope. Going to a party, I would always get a ride so I wouldn't have to drive home, and there I drank, always for the effect. I wouldn't get drunk every time, but drinking made it easier to cope and relate to people, and it took the fear away when I wanted to get next to a chick. Since I couldn't get high, drinking made me feel Not So Straight.

After graduation, four of my classmates and I got summer jobs at a tourist trap in the Rocky Mountains. I had just turned eighteen, and in Colorado, that was the legal age for drinking 3.2 beer. I drank on a daily basis from the first day I arrived. I saw nothing wrong with a *man* getting off work and heading for the bar. I tried to find an Alateen meeting to go to because it was still an important part of my life, but I didn't try very hard, and soon I gave up trying altogether.

One of the guys used to hassle me about drinking so much. I thought, "What does this guy know about it. If anybody is the expert on alcoholism here, I am." So I just ignored him.

One night in the bar with some friends, I was told by them that in the year they had known me, I had never gotten high with them. I should try it again, they said, I would be fun to get high with. It had been close to a month since I had been to an Alateen meeting. Even as I told them about the beauty of the life I had now, I went outside and got high with them. Whatever it was I gained in Alateen, it slipped away, and I couldn't get it back.

In Alateen, I had learned that I am responsible for the way I feel, that no one can make me feel anything I don't want to feel. Being aware of this, I couldn't honestly blame other people for my sudden plunge into the fearful, self-centered, life to which I was returning. I knew in my heart that I couldn't smoke grass and maintain the lifestyle that I so badly wanted, but neither could I leave the dope alone. I would rationalize that the A.A. program had put so much into my head that I was brain washed into thinking I had a problem. Other days, I would be scared and concerned about my lack of self-control. To confront myself I said, "What are you worried about? It's no big deal," or I would make plans to quit, to cut down, to do things to help me get it together. With a joint in my mouth, I didn't get very far. In one of my more self-deceptive moments, I remember writing that my problem was not that I had a problem with grass, but that I worried about it too much. All I had to do was go to more open A.A. meetings, pray more, seldom smoke grass, and I would get over my obsession. I was crazed.

I drank (o.k., so I did black out a few times), but I wasn't obsessed with alcohol as I was with grass. How could I become an alcoholic by smoking dope? I played with this idea for about two years and it never got better for me. I would pray and ask God to release me from the obsession with dope, but down deep I did not even want to stop. I often talked to a guy in A.A., and he asked me about my drinking. I told him that for me alcohol wasn't a problem, but that smoking grass was. The last two years I smoked, I didn't enjoy it. I don't know why, but my stomach tied up in knots if I could not get it. I would pretend that all was well, and the front of being together and cool became more and more important to me. Once again, I would read about the alcoholic in the Big Book, and I could relate on such a gut level that it scared me. I was a *God damn alcoholic.* But where could I get help? I smoked grass, I didn't have a problem with alcohol. I was crazed.

The front itself became a sickness with me. It was so important to me to have people look at me and think that I was a nice-good-looking-mellow-all-together-industrious-guru type and inside I felt like a weak-ugly-frightened-stupid-clumsy nerd. These two personalities became quite distinct in me. They would fight in every quiet moment. The only way I could handle the struggle was to run, sleep, get high, or keep busy. It seemed I was always running, because, more then anything else, I wanted to be able to get high like other people were able to do. Something was wrong with me. I knew it was the disease of alcoholism and that A.A. could help me. In fact, I knew A.A. was my only hope, but I was lost in confusion. How was it possible for me to be an alcoholic, and have marijuana as the obsession? I was crazed.

Determined, I quit again for three months, and things started to clear up for me. The guys I lived with got high all the time, but I seemed to have will power to say, "No, thanks, not today." I was still drinking with them but I felt o.k. about it.

Then came a week's vacation to the mountains with my roommate, and he brought a lid with him. He smoked on the way up, and I had my will power and felt o.k. about not getting high. We got to a small town and was it dead! Absolutely nothing happening. Although the bars were open, I was too young to get in, and I had a terrible feeling of nothing to do, no entertainment, no place to lose myself. I was stuck with me with no way to get away from me. Inside, I panicked. I asked my roommate if he wanted to get high. He replied, "I thought you would." I knew that for me to get high would start the ball rolling again, but now I had no power to stop it. I knew it would be worse than before, bringing back all the trash and bad feeling that I had gotten rid of. I knew all of this, I knew about my problem. I had talked at schools about my problem and prayed and promised myself I would not get high again. No go. I got wasted that night and every day afterwards for about two weeks. After these two weeks I went to my Dad who had been sober ten years and I told him I was getting loaded again. I was hurting and didn't know what to do. After talking to him I made up my mind that I was going to quit again.

The Big Book says that if you don't know that you are an alcoholic, try some controlled drinking. It may be worth a bad case of jitters to gain the true knowledge of your condition. Testing was an excuse to get high once more. Four days later I was loaded before I went to work, and I had said I would never do that. Fear of dying came over me so intensely, I can't describe it. I could see I was killing myself. I hated my guts so much I couldn't stand to look in the mirror. That night a friend in A.A. talked to me and told me about himself. That was the last time I got high, but it was not the end of my drinking.

I knew in my innermost heart that I could not handle drugs. That I was truly powerless over grass and other drugs, I did not doubt, but I felt I could handle booze. If I was careful I wouldn't have any problem with drinking.

I stayed in the same pattern I had always been in since I was twelve. I soon found I was drinking more than I had been, feeling the same feelings of guilt and fear, and hiding the fact that I was drinking from the people closest to me. It was the same as before.

In a short time I realized that I was powerless over all drugs, alcohol included, and that my life was truly unmanageable. I was at a point where I was willing to do anything in this world to get better, to stop living the way I hated so much, but I was trapped. I saw that if I was to keep from killing myself, I needed help. I couldn't do it alone.

Then, a truly amazing thing happened to me, once I admitted that I was an alcoholic. Things began to change. It was as if all other truths were blocked until I faced this truth. Once I was honest about my alcoholism, a world of things unseen about myself opened up. I began to change.

The first several months of my sobriety were not easy for me. I was no longer using the cushion that for so long had protected me from reality. I was left open to feel real feelings, to walk through fear instead of running from it. I was surprised at my degree of self-deception, but this awareness helped me see how really sick I was. A little slogan that helped me through the first few months was "This too shall pass." I believed that if I just stayed clean and sober for one day, it would get better and it did. I started going to a lot of A.A. meetings and, invariably, I would always feel better for having gone. Something in those meetings brought me peace, and God did for me what I could not do for myself. He certainly deserves the credit because it wasn't until I was totally defeated in my struggle for control that I was humble enough to ask God for unconditional help.

The life I was trapped in before A.A. had a very definite direction and destination. As I looked down the road of that life, it contained many things: wrecked cars, hospitals, broken friendships, broken homes, hate, fear, despair, on and on, but worst of all, I had to walk down that road with a person I despised—myself!

The road I am on now has a direction, but I see no end. The only limits I see are the limits I put on it. In God's eyes, it is limitless. It is a joy to be filled with the prospect of learning to live in love, to accept my humanness, and not to feel defeated because of it.

The Twelve Steps of A.A. are tools. They can keep us dry and clean if that's all we want, but sobriety is a never ending process, and if we decide we want more, we can have more at any time. The Twelve Steps worked honestly will keep us on that road—growing and growing and growing.

Amy

To be an alcoholic was tacky.

I grew up in a very close-knit family and experienced a lot of love in my childhood. Drinking was accepted as a social event and liquor was always available. My memory tells me that at age five, I would wake up early in the morning after my parents had had a cocktail party, and I would drink what was left in the glasses from the night before. Although it is vague, this was my first experience with alcohol.

At about eleven years old, my friends took me out to a park with a bottle of Granny's Apple Wine and we got drunk. I liked the taste of the wine, but more than that, I enjoyed the effects. When that bottle came around to me the second time, I held on to it as long as possible and drank as much as possible. Probably it made me feel grown up, or maybe it was that I didn't feel like myself. Whatever it was, I enjoyed what alcohol did to me. It was an escape.

But eleven, even to me, was pretty young to be messing around with alcohol, so I left it alone for the rest of that year. At twelve, however, things began to change. One thing was that I loved swimming and practically lived in a pool. Another was that I started drinking again and by the summer I found myself drunk almost every day. I did a lot of babysitting—usually in the daytime—at that age and because the families I babysat for always seemed to have booze in the house, it was easy to drink under the circumstances. I'd wait until they went out, make sure the child was controllable and get drunk. Sometimes I had a friend with me, but often I did much of my drinking alone. When the parents returned, I'd go over to the pool, swim, and sober up before I went home.

There were a few people who picked up on my behavior and became concerned. I'd promise them I'd never get drunk again, but usually within that same week, the promise was broken. I wasn't really sure what it was that made me drink. Although I didn't enjoy vomiting, hangovers, and the guilt which followed, I continued to get smashed on a regular basis.

During those years I was a competitive swimmer and took it rather seriously, making my main goal to do well in the big meets at the end of the year. That year, when the event was near, I promised my coaches and promised myself that I wouldn't party before the meet. I wanted to do well. Unfortunately, we met at an out-of-town hotel. Someone had bought a case of beer the night before the meet, and I volunteered to keep it in the bath tub of our room until the next night. The booze was there—and suddenly I forgot about the important meet the next day. I had one beer knowing that it wouldn't be enough. Sooner than I thought though, I was drunk. So much for my chances in the big meet the next day. I cried that night—so disappointed in myself that I had failed. I wanted to say no, and I couldn't. It was at that time, somewhere in the back of my mind, I questioned if maybe I had a problem. "Of course not," I convinced myself, "look at your age, and, besides, next time you'll stay sober."

After that summer I attempted to clean up my act. I changed my friends and tried not to think about drinking. Realizing that it was the cause of some of my problems, I tried to limit my drinking to the junior high school parties on weekends, but even that didn't always work out. Once, when I was in eighth grade, I went to a straight slumber party for a girl who was moving away. She didn't serve alcohol at the party, and I couldn't stand it, so doing what I had to, I snuck into her parents' liquor cabinet and began chugging some red wine. Just then, the girl's brother walked in and asked what I was doing. I told him I'd never tasted alcohol before and wanted to see what it was like. It worked, and he kept quiet. Even though my friends were disappointed in me because I was the only one drinking at the party, somehow that didn't matter. Escape was more important than what my friends felt.

Shortly after that, I found myself drinking in situations other than just for kicks. For example, my dog ran away on a rainy day. I skipped school, heading out on my bicycle to look for him, and after searching my neighborhood without finding him, I became depressed. Going home, I knew that my house would be empty at that time of day. Alcohol would ease my pain. And perhaps it did for a short period, but when I sobered up, my dog was still gone and I had my slobbery self to try and live with. It didn't make things better in any way. In fact, it made them worse.

The months passed. One night in the ninth grade I decided to drink because ... well, I just decided to drink. I started in on a large jug of wine and sat alone watching TV downstairs. My parents were home that night, but it was a school night and they didn't come down to check on me. I soon got to the point where I couldn't speak in a clear way. I knew that if I drank that whole jug I'd get sick, but I couldn't stop. Shortly after, I passed out and came to just in time to make it to the toilet and get sick. My parents asked what was wrong; I told them I had the twenty-four hour flu and went to bed. They believed me. Who would expect them not to?

Getting drunk at lunch time made it easier to get through the rest of the school day, but getting home at lunchtime was difficult. So I'd pour liquor into a jar, and keep it in my locker at school. I did this from time to time and finally became a bit concerned about myself. Drunk, I went to the drug counselor at school, because he and I were sort of friends. I told him I was a little concerned about myself, and he told me I was only drinking for attention and not to worry. Naturally my reaction was, "I'll drink to that!" Obviously I was not jumping to accept any help at this time. This behavior continued through the rest of junior high school.

The summer after ninth grade, my family began talking about the possibility of moving. It was painful. I avoided talking about the move, but I didn't avoid drinking about the move. We were to move at the end of summer, and I spent much of that summer drunk, avoiding thinking. When the family moved away, I stayed for an additional week to finish my swimming class. For that week, I lived alone in a house that I was "watching." The picture of myself looked pathetic: drunk every day, alone every night, and scared. That week was the loneliest week of my life. I tried to drink to ease the tension, but booze didn't work as well as it used to. Once again, I decided to turn over a new leaf. When I moved, things were going to be different. I became more honest with myself, but I still wasn't ready to face my real problem.

Once settled in my new home, I promised myself not to drink except on special occasions, and even then I wouldn't get drunk. That lasted till the first party—one week. I got drunk that night, and slipped right back into the old routine. In high school it was easier to drink. *Lots* of kids drank! The difference was that most everyone else didn't always get drunk. I couldn't drink without getting drunk. Something in me couldn't stop.

Once again I found myself smashed when everyone else was straight. It resembled a merry-go-round: drunk in class, drinking alone, drinking in any uncomfortable situation, drinking for no apparent reason, and occasionally drinking in the mornings. People around me began to be more and more concerned, but I was somehow able to make them believe that I was o.k.

I remember going home at lunch time one day, getting drunk, and returning to class. The teacher noticed that something was wrong with me because the next day he confronted me with it. He told me that I acted rather strange in class (he knew I was drunk), but was there anything to worry about? I assured him that I had things under control, though inside I shook and felt scared. The subject was dropped and he didn't tell anyone else about it.

One night, I was at home alone and decided to get drunk. Later that night, there was a knock at the door. He was there. He had come over because he was worried about me, and he said, "You're an alcoholic." I told him never to say that again—and he just stood there looking at me. He began to cry and that really bothered me.

I became resentful when people brought up the subject of my drinking. If it bothered them so much, I'd drink by myself. More and more, I started hiding my drinking, withdrawing into myself. My drinking continued in this way until midway through my junior year in high school when things took a drastic turn.

In one of my classes, I took a forty-questions test which is supposed to help you determine whether or not you have a drinking problem. this is a yes/no test:

Have you ever tried to control your drinking?
Do you have trouble stopping after the first drink?
Do you drink when you're depressed?
Have you ever blacked out?

If you answered any three out of forty yes, you probably had a drinking problem. The first time I took it, I answered sixteen yes. It was then that I went to a teacher friend to talk about my "possible" problem.

After two weeks of talking to me, he tricked me into going to an A.A. meeting. In my view, I went only as an observer, and certainly wouldn't go more than once. I walked into a room of young people who said they were alcoholics. They spoke of their past drinking and how they now had found a way in which they could be happy without alcohol in the program of A.A. The more they talked about themselves, the more I identified, and the more frightened I became. There was *no way* I was an alcoholic (how tacky it was to be an alcoholic) and I was bound and determined to prove that I wasn't. In my need to prove to these people and to myself that I wasn't an alcoholic, I began analyzing myself. I tested myself. I wanted to see if I could go one week without a drink. I couldn't. Three days went by, and I was drinking. I had wanted just one! But here I was, making myself a margarita with the mix I kept between my mattresses, drinking it, fixing another. Everything inside me screamed to pour that second drink down the sink. I knew if I didn't, I didn't have very much (if any) control. I was afraid to take that second drink. I knew I'd hate myself, have the shakes the next morning, have hot and cold sweats all night, but I drank it. I couldn't say no. I couldn't pour it down the sink. It was stronger than I was.

Everything seemed to point to the fact that I was an alcoholic, but there was no way I would believe it. After all, I dressed well, never went to jail, never got in big trouble, never wrecked a car, never lost a job, and could usually handle myself in a somewhat sane manner when I drank. I just couldn't be an alcoholic!

But those people had a lot to offer, and for some reason I kept going back. My parents had no idea that I even had a drinking problem because I made excuses to get to the meetings. The more often I went back, the more I identified with the people—and the worse my drinking got.

At one of the meetings, a man asked me if I thought I might be "a little bit alcoholic." I said, "yes." He then asked me if there was such a thing as being "a little bit pregnant." If I indeed was an alcoholic, time would tell. Things would progress, and somehow I'd know one way or the other. You either are an alcoholic, or you're not. Time would tell.

Time went on and my drinking got worse. I was afraid of the bottle and what it did to me, yet I had to drink. Everytime I drank, it tore me up inside. There was an internal battle going on inside of me, and all I wanted to do was reach the end and decide one way or the other. I didn't want to be an alcoholic and fought being so with everything in my being. This fight went on for about four months.

I reached the point where I couldn't live with alcohol, yet I couldn't live without it. I wanted to give up the fight, but what then? Admit to being an alcoholic? What would my parents say?

One night I reached the point where it didn't matter what my parents thought anymore. All I knew was that I was on the road to self-destruction and something had to change. I couldn't stand the thought of being drunk again. Anything was better than the hell I was experiencing. That night something inside me quit fighting. I could admit, after what seemed like a ten-year battle, that alcohol was stronger than I was. I Was An Alcoholic. I was an alcoholic, and it *was* o.k. I could learn to live without alcohol. I was on the road to recovery.

Sobriety has in no way been a bowl of cherries, but no one promised me that it would be. My disease was difficult for my parents to accept and those first few months of sobriety were quite hard. After being in A.A. for a short while, I went back out and drank again twice. Both times my disease worsened and I saw that alcoholism is progressive. I was fortunate to get back to A.A.

I haven't found it necessary to take a drink for about a year now, and life is definitely one hundred and ten percent better than when I drank. Thanks to my Higher Power and the love of the people around, I've been able to look at myself and at my disease. There have been tough times, but there was nothing God and I couldn't handle together. My worst day sober is still much better than my best one drunk. Being an alcoholic *is* o.k. if I decide to recover. I've found a Program full of love and learning. One day at a time I don't take a drink; one day at a time life gets better.

The Twelve Steps of Alcoholics Anonymous

1. We admitted we were powerless over alcohol—that our lives had become unmanageable.
2. Came to believe that a Power greater than ourselves could restore us to sanity.
3. Made a decision to turn our will and our lives over to the care of God *as we understood Him.*
4. Made a searching and fearless moral inventory of ourselves.
5. Admitted to God, to ourselves, and to another human being, the exact nature of our wrongs.
6. Were entirely ready to have God remove all these defects of character.
7. Humbly asked Him to remove our shortcomings.
8. Made a list of all persons we had harmed, and became willing to make amends to them all.
9. Made direct amends to such people wherever possible, except when to do so would injure them or others.
10. Continued to take personal inventory and when we were wrong promptly admitted it.
11. Sought through prayer and meditation to improve our conscious contact with God *as we understood Him,* praying only for knowledge of His will for us and the power to carry that out.
12. Having had a spiritual awakening as the result of these steps, we tried to carry this message to alcoholics, and to practice these principles in all our affairs.

The Twelve Steps of Narcotics Anonymous

1. We admitted that we were powerless over our addiction, that our lives had become unmanageable.
2. We came to believe that a power greater than ourselves could restore us to sanity.
3. We made a decision to turn our will and our lives over to the care of God *as we understood Him.*
4. We made a searching and fearless moral inventory of ourselves.
5. We admitted to God, to ourselves, and to another human being the exact nature of our wrongs.
6. We were entirely ready to have God remove all these defects of character.
7. We humbly asked Him to remove our shortcomings.
8. We made a list of all persons we had harmed, and became willing to make amends to them all.
9. We made direct amends to such people wherever possible, except when to do so would injure them or others.
10. We continued to take personal inventory, and when we were wrong promptly admitted it.
11. We sought through prayer and meditation to improve our conscious contact with God, *as we understood Him,* praying only for knowledge of His will for us, and the power to carry that out.
12. Having had a spiritual awakening as a result of these steps, we tried to carry this message to addicts and to practice these principles in all our affairs.

The Palmer Drug Abuse Program

1. We admitted that mind-changing chemicals had caused at least part of our lives to become unmanageable.
2. We found it necessary to "Stick with Winners" in order to grow.
3. We realized that a Higher Power, expressed through our love for each other, can help restore us to sanity.
4. We made a decision to turn our will and our lives over to the care of God, as we understand Him.
5. We made a searching and fearless moral inventory of ourselves.
6. We admitted to God, to ourselves, and to another human being the exact nature of our wrongs.
7. We became willing to allow our Higher Power, through the Love of the group, to help change our way of life and humbly asked Him to help us change.
8. We made a list of all persons we had harmed and became willing to make amends to them all.
9. We made direct amends to such people, whenever possible, except when to do so would injure them, others or ourselves.
10. We have continued to look at ourselves and when wrong, promptly admitted it.
11. We have sought through prayer and meditation to improve our conscious contact with our Higher Power, that we have chosen to call God, praying only for knowledge of His Will for us and courage to carry that out.
12. We, having had a Spiritual awakening as a result of these Steps, tried to carry our love and understanding to others, and to practice these principles in our daily lives.

More ideas from young people, for young people ...

Feed Your Head
Some Excellent Stuff on Being Yourself
written by Earl Hipp, illustrated by L. K. Hanson
Survive and thrive during the teen years! With an irreverent touch—and lots of humor—the graphic survival guide for those ages 11 to 17 creates a map for handling crises, depression, responsibility, and changing feelings about parents, friends, and self. 137 pp.
Order No. 5034

Hazelden Step Pamphlets for Young Adults
Easy to read and write in, these workbook-style guides to the first five Steps of recovery provide a solid core of Twelve Step understanding. Each workbook explains how alcohol or other drugs can affect you, then asks you to think about your own situation.

- Step One for Young Adults
  Order No. 1362

- Step Two for Young Adults
  Order No. 5501

- Step Three for Young Adults
  Order No. 5502

- Step Four for Young Adults
  Order No. 1129

- Step Five for Young Adults
  Order No. 5505

- **Workbook Collection**
  Order No. 0828
  All five workbooks
